Memorial Services

The new Alcuin Liturgy Guides series revives the tradition of the Alcuin Manual. The Guides are essentially concerned with the practice of liturgy, its setting and celebration. The aim is to publish two Liturgy Guides in alternate years, following the publication of books of liturgical scholarship and commentary, the so-called Alcuin Collection.

The projected topics for the new Liturgy Guides series include the celebration of the Eucharist; children, communion and confirmation; music in worship; and the use of liturgical symbols in worship. The majority of these titles will consider the new rites and services of *Common Worship*, and together will, to all intents, form a third volume of the *Companion to Common Worship*. The series editor is the Revd Christopher Irvine.

Members of the Alcuin Club receive free copies of the Collection, Liturgy Guides, and the Joint Liturgical Studies. The Alcuin Club promotes the study of Christian liturgy, especially the liturgy of the Anglican Communion, and its chairman is Dr Donald Gray CBE. Details of membership may be obtained from the Revd Tim Barker, The Parsonage, 8 Church Street, Spalding, Lincolnshire PE11 2PB.

Memorial Services

Donald Gray

Alcuin Liturgy Guides 1

Published in Great Britain 2002 by
Society for Promoting Christian Knowledge
Holy Trinity Church
Marylebone Road
London NW1 4DU

British Library Cataloguing-in-Publication Data
A catalogue record for this book is available from the British Library

ISBN 0–281–05406–1

Typeset by Wilmaset Ltd, Birkenhead, Wirral
Printed in Great Britain by
Antony Rowe Ltd, Chippenham, Wiltshire

Contents

For the St Margaret's team:
Pamela, Harold, Nigel, Simon C,
Simon O and Thomas;
companions in 157
Memorial Services.

Preface

I am grateful to my colleagues on the Alcuin Club Committee for entrusting to me the authorship of this the first of our new series of Alcuin Liturgy Guides. No doubt they believed that, having arranged, compiled and conducted just over a hundred and fifty Memorial Services at St Margaret's during my time at Westminster Abbey, I might have a little wisdom to impart on the subject.

I have indeed drawn on that experience and I am grateful to the Dean and Chapter of Westminster for allowing me to reproduce material which is their copyright. Additionally Pamela Carrington, Nigel Harris, Christine Smith and Dr Tony Trowles have been extremely helpful in hunting out items of importance.

Others have also been generous with their information and I would particularly thank Dr Chris Pond (House of Commons Library), David Skidmore (Board of Social Responsibility of the Archbishops' Council), Canon Brian Hebblethwaite (Queens' College, Cambridge), Canon John Andrew (New York) and the Very Revd Dr Wesley Carr (Dean of Westminster).

Andrew Barr has been especially kind in commenting on the contents of this guide and allowing me to see, and use, his thoughts on the service at Dunblane.

Some few years ago, in Westminster, we held a series of useful discussions on the subject of Memorial Services. I have recalled the substance of some of them and the Very Revd Michael Mayne and Canon Geoffrey Brown will recognize their contributions to those debates.

The Revd Dr Paul Sheppy most helpfully read the opening chapters; the Revd Christopher Irvine (the Editorial Secretary of the Alcuin Club) has been supportive throughout, while the Revd Michael Thompson very kindly undertook the task of reading and commenting on the whole text. Ruth McCurry at SPCK has been a patient editor.

My wife, Joyce, has once again coped with putting my disordered manuscript into a neat typescript. We would both like to be associated with the heartfelt dedication of this guide.

Donald Gray
Stamford, Lincolnshire
St Barnabas Day, 2001

Acknowledgements

Permission to reproduce memorial services for the Rt Revd and Rt Hon. the Lord Runcie and Eric Samuel Heffer has been granted by the Dean and Chapter of Westminster, with the agreement of Lady Runcie and Mrs Doris Heffer. The Dean and Chapter of Southwark gave permission to reproduce the memorial service after the disaster on Sunday, 20 August 1989 on the River Thames. The assistance of the Revd Colin McIntosh and the Parents Group at Dunblane is gratefully acknowledged. I also acknowledge the kindness of the Revd Dr Peter Mullen in allowing me to quote his *Spectator* article of 21 April 2001, Thomas Lynch from his *Times* review of Richard P. Taylor, *Death and the Afterlife* (23 May 2001) and Alan Bennett for a quotation from *The Laying on of Hands*. The material for memorial services from *Common Worship: Services and Prayers for the Church of England* is copyright © The Archbishops' Council 2000.

Every effort has been made to trace and acknowledge the copyright holders of material reproduced in this book. The publishers apologize for any omissions and, if notified, will ensure that full acknowledgements are made in a subsequent edition.

Chapter 1

The Memorial Service – What Is It?

This guide is intended as a 'how to do it' book, not a volume of reminiscences of services conducted or attended. I have therefore tried to make it as practical as possible realizing the danger thus involved of seeming, too often, to be stating the obvious or providing over-meticulous directions. For this I apologize, pleading that I believed it better to err on the side of providing too much detail rather than too little, leaving readers to decide what they find useful and to discard the rest. As Percy Dearmer said, in the most famous of Anglican 'how to do it' books, *The Parson's Handbook*:

> Everyone who writes about ceremonial is certain to be subject to one or two forms of criticism; either that his directions are too minute, or that they are not minute enough.
>
> The answer to the first objection is plain in a practical book of this kind. No one is bound to follow them: it is safer, therefore, to give too many directions than too few. Half an hour with a blue pencil will reduce the ceremonial to the required simplicity; but faults of omission would take much longer to rectify.
>
> Furthermore, there is undoubtedly a right and a wrong way of doing everything, and therefore it is just as well to do things in the right way; for unless one has an unusually large share of instinctive grace and tact, one will otherwise be in danger of making oneself, and also the service one is conducting (which is more important), appear uncouth, or queer, or ridiculous.

One further word of explanation. I have to admit that my most recent experience has been of arranging services for 'the great and the good', but I trust that does not mean that the advice and suggestions I have made in this guide are entirely inappropriate for less grand occasions. I believe that every service, and consequently every mourning family, deserves the most careful attention to detail. All are equally important.

Throughout this guide the term 'memorial service' has been used as convenient shorthand for the more popular titles such as 'A Service of Thanksgiving for the Life and Work of N'. No judgement on alternative titles is intended by this usage.

It has to be acknowledged that the form and nature which memorial services have now taken are not without trenchant critics. Some services are said to be sentimental, if not downright dishonest. The Revd Dr Peter Mullen who as Rector of St Michael's Cornhill and Chaplain to the Stock Exchange has been involved in many services in the City of London, believes that many occasions these days plumb new depths of banality. They are not just wordy; Dr Mullen accuses them of being talkative.

> New-style memorial services are, above all, talkative. Three or even four of the deceased's family and friends will get up to 'offer a tribute'. I know we must all respect *De mortuis nil nisi bonum*, but these tributes would fall foul of the Trades Descriptions Act. We are asked to recall that Bob, 'or Chuckles, as he liked to be called on account of his infectious giggle', was a married archangel with four children and 15 grandchildren. He was brilliant at his work at the bank where everybody loved him. At home he had the bonhomie of Alastair Sim playing the reformed Scrooge. He kept a superb table, never failed to bring his wife flowers every Friday and he was always effervescently happy. Well, Solon said, 'Call no man happy until he's dead', but I hardly thought he meant that a man had to wait until after he'd died to effect such a remarkable character change – from an ordinary man, with ordinary virtues and vices, to a paragon of virtue. I suppose it's a blessing that most of the speakers haven't the faintest notion of how to project the voice, and so the sentimental drivel cannot be heard at all beyond the third row.

Of such occasions, Mullen declares, 'Frankly I'd rather forget.'

Thomas Lynch is a rare combination of poet, essayist and funeral director. Writing in *The Times* he is critical of the fact that we seem to be moving towards a situation in which funeral services are entirely replaced by memorial services. Increasingly the newspaper announcement of a death contains no details of the funeral, only of a memorial service. Lynch says,

> Of course nowadays, as often as not, the dead are nowhere to be found at their funerals. The dead body had been summarily dispatched by cellphone and credit card and some tidy professional, as the 'barbaric', least convenient, manifestly dysfunctional, user-friendly reminder of our own mortality, now unwelcome at its own obsequies which we have renamed a 'Service of Thanksgiving' or 'Celebration of Life' or some similarly upmarket, emotively neutered, and tastefully predictable 'Memorial Cocktail Soirée'. We do not so much 'deal' with our dead as disappear them.

However, this guide is not dealing with a service which *replaces* a funeral. The services under discussion are in *addition* to a funeral, a few weeks or even months later. Those services of which Harold Macmillan said, 'I rather agree with Ralph Richardson that memorial services are the "cocktail parties of the geriatric set" '.

It would seem that in the United States, Canada and Australia the term is used both for services to replace a funeral and also for an additional service. But in these countries such an additional occasion usually follows hard on the heels of the funeral and is rarely the elaborate affair to which we are becoming accustomed in England (and sometimes Scotland).

This guide accepts that there are memorial services in England which might be viewed as less than satisfactory from a number of points of view and which might have been better restyled as 'memorial meetings' and held in a secular place. For instance when *The Times* or the *Telegraph* describes a service which is no more than a concert. This is particularly true if there is any association with show business. A recent service in St Paul's, Covent Garden contained readings from *Molloy* by Samuel Beckett, *At the Abbey Theatre* by W. B. Yeats, *Amongst Women* by John O'Donohue. There were five tributes (including one which had been pre-recorded and then played to the congregation over the loud speaker system). Songs were sung: 'Finnegan's wake' from 'Mr Joyce is Leaving Paris' and 'Nora' from *The Plough and the Stars*; the deceased's son played 'Fly away' on the guitar and a violinist 'Danny Boy'. All of which paled into insignificance when the recorded voice of the dear departed was heard in a quartet singing 'Leaning on a lamppost'. However, such histrionic occasions do not invalidate this form of commemoration, which we call a memorial service, and ought only to make us redouble our efforts to maintain, or even raise, standards.

The Roman Catholic Church has, as yet, managed to hold back the intrusion of these elements into its services, but the 'Memorial Mass' is alive and well in England. These are once-for-all occasions; they are not the month's or year's minds – the anniversary masses of the Roman Missal. It is convenient for our newspapers that in their accounts of such Masses it is possible to record the readers of lections, the leaders of the general intercessions and the givers of the tributes, thus producing an account in the press similar to the memorial services of other denominations. Thus honour is served all round.

It remains true that the form of memorial services is still very free, and although this guide is not intended to lay down any hard and fast rules about either their shape or their contents, it is mainly concerned with standards. The possibilities for their contents are enormous and we have avoided detailed suggestions. To supply that need would have required a book three times the size of this. However, the bibliography provides details of books that contain such suggestions. Their use can perhaps avoid the temptation, for some, of blindly copying the contents of the last service attended!

In addition Chapter 6 contains four actual services that have taken place in recent years: two for individuals and two after tragic events. These 'exemplars' are accompanied by a commentary. It is hoped that they will be of help.

It is our firm conviction that the Church must take seriously these services because they meet people where they are. It is an ideal opportunity to serve those who do not regularly cross the threshold of our churches in a particular hour of need. Not to take advantage of their distress – but to serve humbly. If, at every stage, they are met by courtesy, sensitivity and a discreet professionalism, then who knows what the effect of that might be. Reactions to our offer to minister in this way will vary enormously: some may be merely nostalgic, others frankly cathartic. Another article in the secular press was perhaps surprisingly insightful beneath its attempt to be light-hearted:

> In the wealthy secular Western world, death is kept at a distance and grief is a private weakness. The graveside scene with its healing catharsis is now the stuff of melodrama. Yet society needs to farewell its treasured members; individuals need to square accounts, to say the unsaid and, sometimes, to unsay the regretted. As Dame Maggie Smith said wistfully after the theatrical establishment told Larry it loved him: 'I wish he had been there. It was thrilling.' (*Tatler*, March 1992)

Despite all these criticisms, it cannot be denied that memorial services (or Services of Thanksgiving) do provide enormous pastoral opportunities. Some might question the advisability of the time lapse which occurs between the funeral and such a service. 'Is it kind to the mourners?' it may be asked. Might it not be thought to be 'dragging it all up again'? That does not seem to be the case.

A speculation: Part of the clue as to why these services are successful and appreciated might be found in the desire to call them a 'Service of Thanksgiving'. They are certainly not miserable occasions, there is genuine thanksgiving in them. So could it be that, in an oblique way, those involved are participating in a form of resurrection joy? Perhaps that is fanciful, but God is good and has love for all his children. It is worth repeating that there is a worthwhile ministry for the Church in the memorial service, and we ought not to be mealy-mouthed or patronizing about them. They deserve careful planning, sensitive help and guidance in the selection of the elements to be included in the service; indeed they need from us the highest degree of pastoral and liturgical care. 'Where charity and love are, there is God.'

Chapter 2

History and Development

Discreet funerals and extravagant memorial services are not unusual these days, the finality of death mitigated by staggering it over two stages. 'Of course there'll be a memorial service,' people say, excusing their non-attendance at the emotionally more demanding (and socially less enjoyable) obsequies. And it is generally the case nowadays that anybody who is anybody is accorded a memorial service – and sometimes an anybody who isn't.

Alan Bennett, The Laying on of Hands

Whatever church attendance statistics claim they can reveal about changing patterns of Christian worship in the twenty-first century, there is, undeniably, one notable and significant point of liturgical growth. There have emerged, over the past 30 years, particular occasions when our churches have been found to be at their fullest. These new church-filling experiences are what are known, in England at least, as memorial services.

The present-day vitality of this increasingly common liturgical form can be seen by opening one of the broadsheet newspapers any morning. Turn to the 'Court Page' and there you will see on most days a good deal of space devoted to them, in the form of either announcements of services or reports of the previous day's occasions. There is naturally a slight lull each year in high summer, but the notifications quickly pick up when folk are back from their summer holidays in September. As well as the announcements telling of a coming event there is very often a cryptic phrase added at the end of the immediate death notices. It is something on the lines of: 'a memorial service will be held later'. This is intended as a broad hint that, in these circumstances, the vast majority of the acquaintances of the departed do not need to upset their plans, and rapidly move appointments around in order to get to a funeral at an awkward time; they will be able to attend another service later with considerably less personal inconvenience.

Are not these memorial services normally for the allegedly great and good? Are we not talking about honouring departed members of the higher echelons of society? Perhaps 20 or more years ago that would have been true. No, the pattern of a family-only funeral which is followed, at a distance of what might be up to two or three months by a memorial service, is fast becoming a firmly common pattern. Go back to those so-called Court Pages and you will see that the services advertised there these days are a mixture of those to be held in memory of people who have made a modest, but perhaps not necessarily highly significant, contribution to our national life, alongside services announced for 'the Captains and the Kings' of industry, commerce, politics, diplomacy, culture and the arts. Many of the listed services, even in the national press, are perforce of only local or regional interest, but certainly no less significant because of that.

Additionally there are now frequent requests, in more modest circumstances, for a service of memorial which is quite separate from the funeral service.

At the time of the *Alternative Service Book* no special thought was given to suggesting any material for these services; where necessary local initiative was to be relied upon. However, the rapid growth of this form of observance has necessitated the more recently authorized *Common Worship* to be proactive on the subject and two outline orders are offered for guidance within its provisions. The first is the general form which might be expected, while the second provides for a memorial service within a Celebration of the Holy Communion – a Requiem (p. 332). *Common Worship: Pastoral Services* also contains a more detailed 'sample service' for a memorial service (p. 335). The notes preceding this material mention the possibility of a memorial service being held on the same day as the funeral, or very soon after, and suggests that if that is so the order to be followed should be that of the Funeral Service, without the committal. In her guide to *Common Worship* funerals, R. Anne Horton comments that if funeral and memorial services are held fairly closely together in this way, 'The Minister and family may feel a complete duplication of the Funeral Service would not help the bereaved family move on through the grief process' (Horton, 2000, pp. 98–99). Horton thinks they might prefer the service to be more a mixture of funeral service and memorial service. In other words, because the funeral has already happened this subsequent service must not have a structure which is seemingly moving towards a climax in the act of committal.

The need for other post-funeral services is also recognized in Horton's guide to the *Common Worship* services. She mentions annual memorial services, such as on All Souls' Day, and suggests the use at these of material contained in *The Promise of His Glory*. However, there is evidence of a growing number of requests for a special service on the precise anniversary of a death. This is particularly traditional in some cultures, such as the Afro-Caribbean, but is also occurring more widely. To supply this need the ecumenical Joint Liturgical Group (JLG) is preparing material for such services which they entitle 'Remembrance of those who have died, on the anniversary of their death'. Additionally JLG is to publish 'An Affirmation of the Living'. This service is intended for use by those who perceive that their period of grieving after bereavement is now over and ask God's blessing on fashioning new schemes and plans 'after the death of partner, parents or children'. The Group has in mind those who have come to realize that God is in the future just as surely as he is in the past.

HISTORICAL BACKGROUND

The genesis of memorial services is to be discovered in the nineteenth-century custom of arranging parallel commemorations in provincial churches on the day of the funeral of royalty or the particularly famous. These events also occurred in London if the funeral itself was in Windsor or elsewhere outside the capital. The services were often accompanied by street processions which were a popular spectacle and consequently attracted large crowds.

John Wolffe has researched the development of parallel services in *Great Deaths: Grieving, Religion and Nationhood in Victorian and Edwardian Britain* (2000). He maintains that the precedent for such services was set at the time of the calamitous death of Princess Charlotte, the 20-year-old only child of George IV and heir to the throne, in 1817. It was an occurrence of widespread national mourning. Wolffe says that although in the next 30 years parallel memorial services were few, yet throughout the country after the death of a notable personage special funeral sermons would be preached on an appropriate Sunday during the statutory services. The one exception in this barren period was the numerous and well-attended local commemorations held to coincide with the funeral of Wellington at St Paul's Cathedral in 1852. Nine years later, on the sudden death of the Prince Consort, even these numbers were greatly exceeded. It would seem that there were services in all churches and most non-conformist chapels on the day of Prince Albert's funeral. In subsequent years the funerals of politicians such as Palmerston and Disraeli occasioned a more limited level of observance, but a commemoration no less.

The earliest memorial service for non-royalty in Westminster Abbey seems to have been that for Charles Kingsley in 1875; his funeral and burial having taken place at Eversley, Hampshire. In 1885 there were services in the Abbey and St Paul's for General Gordon which were mirrored in cathedrals and churches throughout the country. It was reported that on this occasion congregations often overflowed into the churchyard. That same year the Abbey held a service, less than a fortnight after his death, 'In Memory of General Grant, Late President of the United States'.

The next quarter of a century provides many examples of parallel memorial services, so much so that there began to be concern in ecclesiastical circles over the content of such services. The Church was in the midst of a period of considerable liturgical tension arising out of the ritualistic controversies of the time. One of the points of the greatest contention in these debates involved the propriety of praying for the dead. The authorities were anxious lest any of these new-fangled services seemed to contain such a dangerous element. In order to regulate matters on the death of Queen Victoria two official forms of service were issued; one containing the litany, parts of the burial office and special prayers; the other was an amalgamation of parts of the burial service with Morning Prayer and some suggestions for suitable music. The service was for use on the day of the Queen's funeral 'or on a convenient day within the Octave'.

Wolffe gives many examples of large crowds drawn to parallel memorial services in the nineteenth and early twentieth centuries. He comments, 'The indications, moreover, are that many of those normally on the fringes of organised religion found the combination of patriotism, a sense of occasion, and emotional hymn-singing, a powerful magnet drawing them to relatively unaccustomed participation in public worship' (Wolffe (2000), p. 93).

Although some of the public reaction to the death of Winston Churchill in 1965 has been compared to that at the time of the funeral of the Duke of Wellington, this was mainly represented by general approval of the splendid ceremonial which accompanied his obsequies. There were few local commemorations for Churchill. Whereas the death of Diana, Princess of Wales in 1997 did generate many local services and, most notably, an explosion of shrines, places of pilgrimage (some of which attracted an almost overwhelming avalanche of flowers, teddy bears, messages and mementoes). Most recently the tragic events in New York and Washington immediately stimulated in Great Britain many special services of a greater or lesser formality. These services all seemed to have one common element – the lighting of candles. This gesture, borrowed from Christian piety (and that of a decidedly 'catholic' nature), seems to have become the prime private or public symbol of remembrance in cases of tragic loss in the twenty-first century.

The emergence of the type of memorial service with which this guide is concerned is as recent as the 1960s. It was then that services for artists, sportsmen and more household names begin to appear. Only a brief examination of the names of those commemorated in this way makes plain that men were in the vast majority of those being thus honoured. There is one particular development however in contrast to 40 years ago: today's press notices announce services to be conducted not only in our cathedrals and major parish churches but also in churches and chapels, large and small, up and down the country. These services are not just for a distinguished elite – and women are beginning to take their rightful place among the memorialized.

Thus the definition of a memorial service as being 'a funeral service without a coffin' is, in the main, a firmly late twentieth-century concept. Perusal of the Alcuin Club bibliography will reveal the existence of an earlier publication entitled *Memorial Services.* This was one of the Club's Prayer Book Revision Pamphlets (*Memorial Services*, 1914). Its contents, which it acknowledged have been extracted from *A Prayer Book Revised,* an anonymous set of proposals for Prayer Book revision published in 1913 (almost certainly by Percy Dearmer, with a preface by Charles Gore), bear no relation to the type of services under consideration in this guide. The services it contains are merely intended as developments of the 1662 Prayer Book funeral rites. The Alcuin Club recognizes that the needs of the Church of the twenty-first century are vastly different, and hence this publication.

In this guide we shall also discuss the increasing number of requests for a form of worship which is now also termed 'a memorial service'. These are services held subsequent to an accident or tragedy. As we shall discover these services have features which are common to the post-funeral occasion we have already examined and others which are of necessity quite different.

It is a surprising fact that recent literature on Christian interpretations of death do not seem to have noticed the growth of memorial services. Professor Douglas J. Davies of the Department of Theology at the University of Durham might be described as a 'sociologist of death'. His detailed and acute observations of what occurs at the time of death; what people do at the time of bereavement; what rituals they find helpful and comforting; what 'words against death' seem to be supportive: all are carefully delineated in his definitive *Death, Ritual and Belief: The Rhetoric of Funerary Rites* (1997) without any mention of the phenomenon of the memorial service.

More recently David Edwards has left us in his debt for his *After Death? Past Beliefs and Real Possibilities* (2001). Yet Dr Edwards similarly fails to recognize the significance of the present-day growth of the memorial service. During his discussion of what he calls a 'revolution in funerary customs', Edwards rightly emphasizes a growing dislike by many for the 'fuss' of the graveyard burial which is the result of a decline in familiarity with church buildings and the clergy, and a decline in belief in a future 'resurrection of the body' (p. 20). He does this without going on to link the dislike and seeming dissatisfaction with the traditional rite and the twentieth-century evolvement of the memorial service which folk believe can have the consequential effect of alleviating some of that fuss.

Chapter 3

Pastoral Considerations

What has brought about this change of funerary patterns? There are a number of factors. It is probable that the 'convenience' angle, which we have already noted, is one major consideration. No cynicism is implied by listing this as an issue affecting any decision regarding the pattern of post-death arrangements. In most circumstances, travel is now quicker and easier. This has the advantage that the immediate members of a family can, in an emergency, arrive from a distance in time for an early funeral. Whereas the congregation for the modern, what I dare to call 'social', memorial service is drawn from a large proportion of people for whom such urgent measures would not seem at all appropriate. The need to attend the service is, in these cases, important but not crucial, and anyway the attendance of a 'representative' will often be deemed equally appropriate. Certainly it is a fact that the list of those attending, whether as proxies or in their own right, is studied with the greatest interest by both family, friends, colleagues – and the general newspaper-reading public.

There is another factor which, in the 'social' category, usually influences the wide separation of the funeral service with its subsequent burial or, more frequently, cremation from a more public and crowded memorial service. It is popularly perceived as being sympathetic to the sensitivities of the bereaved family to leave the immediate ceremonies, that is the funeral service and the committal, for them to conduct in private. Additionally after the death, the family themselves often express the wish to mourn privately; choosing to have only those closest to them present while they perform, as they see it, the intimate and necessary tasks of commendation and committal. Tears can then be shed in private and black can be worn with impunity at this juncture.

This banishment of public grief and privatization of mourning has inevitably had an effect on the nature and contents of the subsequent memorial service, as we shall discuss later. It is usually desired that the later service avoids any overemphasis on mourning – that having been a dominant theme of the funeral rite – and a note of thanksgiving is preferred.

There is another important, often unspoken, reason for the emergence of this modern pattern of a twofold commemoration in these cases. If the memorial service is to be the major *public* commemoration of the departed it can reflect the degree of religious faith (or the paucity of it) of the deceased. The authorized and traditional funeral rites of the Christian Church are designed and intended to be used without equivocation (or amendment) as the final rites for those who espouse the Faith. Equally they are meant to give Christian comfort, assurance and hope to those taking part in them. For instance the 1662 Book of Common Prayer service is conducted in 'sure and certain hope' of the resurrection. All subsequent revisions across the divides of Christendom are equally definite in their Christian confidence.

Writing of the Roman Catholic *Order of Christian Funerals* (1989) Richard Rutherford writes for all Christians when he says: 'The Christian funeral is, above all, a celebration of the paschal mystery, a profession of faith in the hope of sharing Jesus' own resurrection to fullness of life in God' (Rutherford, 1990, pp. 122–23). Of that funeral Rutherford declares that it proclaims in word and sacrament that life in the Christ of the paschal mystery does not end with human death but extends into the eternal present of God's kingdom beyond death. This is made unambiguously clear in the introduction to the *Order of Christian Funerals* when it states:

> It is the paschal mystery of Christ that the Church confidently celebrates in the funerals of its children, for those who through baptism have been incorporated into the body of Christ dead and risen pass with him through death to life – their souls purified and taken into heaven with the saints; their bodies meanwhile awaiting the blessed hope of Christ's coming and the resurrection of the dead.

In his commentary on the revised rites of the Roman Catholic Church, Fr Rutherford underlines the fact that 'paschal mystery' and 'everlasting life' are not merely images that lend a Christian flavour to the coping rituals and grief therapy of people who happen to call themselves Christians. They are images which proclaim the very bedrock of the Christian faith. These are sentiments which would be echoed by commentators from other Christian churches.

It is a barely disguised fact that, regrettably, a significant proportion of those for whom a memorial service is likely to be requested would not have been able in their lifetime to make such a definitive statement of faith. Equally, not all grieving families would be able to affirm similar convictions. Consequently they would not necessarily have cast all their care on God, nor have known the consolation of his love (*ASB*, p. 335). Michael Perham has stated that in the recent past, much of the Church of England's provisions have been 'light years away from where most mourners are' (Jupp and Rogers, 1997, p. 157).

This is not to suggest that the Church should impose any kind of 'faith test' before deciding whether they can or cannot offer a funeral service, or even a memorial service. There were some such bizarre attempts in the nineteenth century by certain zealous Tractarians. Not surprisingly, they always proved to be pastorally disastrous. For example, some clergy believed they had discovered a rubrical loophole by which they could avoid taking the bodies of those whom they judged as being 'ungodly livers' into Church. Instead they directed that the cortège should go directly to the grave side. They justified this by quoting the Prayer Book rubric: 'The Priest and Clerks meeting the corpse at the entry of the Church-yard . . . going before it, either into the Church, or towards the grave'. No such arbitrary decisions are even vaguely conceivable today. What a field day the press would have!

The new funeral services in *Common Worship* have the avowed aim of being grounded in common experience. Critics of the *Alternative Service Book* funeral rite allege that the opening prayer, declaring that those present have 'a true faith and a sure hope', a faith and hope which inspires us to live as those who believe in the resurrection to eternal life, is generally inappropriate at the beginning of the service (see *ASB*, p. 308). The task Perham believes is to lead people some way towards such an expression of faith by the end of the service, whereas at the beginning of the service people are 'fragile, worried whether they will cope with the next half hour, let alone life for years ahead' (Jupp and Rogers, 1977, pp. 130–42).

Both because of, or even despite, these considerations there is still a large constituency of those who desire to have, as the major commemoration of their departed, a ceremony which can still be perceived as religious. They wish it to be held in a Christian place of worship, but increasingly they are anxious that the service should be tailored to suit the faith level that they believe to be appropriate both to their own circumstances and in regard to that of the deceased. Any possibility of leaving the gate open to an accusation of that heinous sin hypocrisy is thus avoided. The problem only remains to find ingredients for such a ceremony which may be deemed suitable, yet preserves sufficient religious neutrality so as not to be an embarrassment on the day. This is seldom successfully achieved. There is sometimes a further problem created by an ambition to provide a 'bigger and better' service or at least 'as good as' a recent occasion involving a friend, colleague or even rival. It is not unknown for an aura of competition to surround the proceedings, even at this late stage of what is not even life.

Yet it is essential, in the final analysis, that all those involved remember that the service is a Christian act of worship in a building dedicated to that purpose. This is the faith which has caused it to be built and it is the professed faith of those who today lovingly maintain it as an expression of that belief. Consequently its present-day custodians are entitled to insist on expressing that faith in anything that happens within the building, even if those beliefs are not always shared by all the participants on any particular occasion. The hypocrisy argument does not arise; to have a clear and explicit Christian event in such a building is only to be expected. If any of those present do not share that faith, the service is not thereby invalidated. The only caveat is that those custodians must not automatically assume that their faith is shared and carelessly include declarations (particularly in prayers) that seem to make that assumption.

Mourning is always a process and the funeral service however carefully arranged and delicately and perceptively conducted cannot do everything that is needed for those who grieve. Yet it can provide a map. Dr Paul Sheppy, the Baptist liturgical scholar, has suggested that a memorial service can be part of that map for some people. In the same way, some Christians find a Requiem Mass cathartic while others do not. The memorial service (or Service of Thanksgiving) must be part of the Church's ministerial and pastoral outreach at the time of death, one of the items it can offer among a range of possibilities.

SERVICES AFTER DISASTER AND TRAGEDIES

We have already made passing reference to the sad fact that there are other rather different, and tragic, circumstances which necessitate what is also termed a memorial service. Once again it appears that such a way of marking these tragedies by the holding of a church service is on the increase. Even in an age which is regularly described as faithless, when sadly these awful occasions occur, there is general agreement that a service should be organized.

A recent report, *Guidelines for Faith Communities when Dealing with Disasters* (1997), has concluded that in these circumstances 'There is likely to be an expectation that some of the faith communities will organise a formal, large-scale memorial service', thus providing an opportunity for those affected by the disaster to share their grief with others. The report is of the opinion that 'services of this kind can provide a focus for the grief and anger of the wider community, not just those affected by the disaster'. Given that such an occasion will often have local, even national attention, and consequential media coverage 'the organisation and structure of such events need to be considered very carefully, covering such aspects as timing, invitation and conduct' (*Guidelines*, 1997, p. 21).

However, we should not allow this appearance of apparent consensus to obscure the evidence. In contemporary society a very large number of people do not automatically find a church, chapel or cathedral service capable of serving their deeply felt needs. In recent years what may well be termed 'folk religion' has tended quickly to organize its own ceremonies in the immediate aftermath of tragedy. The disasters at Hillsborough and Heysel, for example, produced similar manifestations of corporate grieving as did the sudden and accidental death of the Princess of Wales. It is fascinating to observe that on each of these terrible occasions the general instinct was to use objects and devices that are usually identified with orthodox religious worship.

There is also the importance of location. Having rejected a normal place of worship the choice has been, for instance, a football ground which immediately evokes memories of comradeship and esprit de corps. Or, as we recall, in the case of the Princess, it was a royal palace which served as a tangible reminder of regal mystery and splendour. This implicit popular importance of location can also be seen in the need to provide the rapidly erected shrines of flowers and messages at the site of road and rail accidents and acts of violence, shootings and killings. The articles of devotion that are presented at these larger or smaller shrines are quickly recognizable as being the equivalent to those used by the faithful at traditional places of religious devotion: candles, flowers and votive offerings. It is noteworthy to observe the need of many 'protestant' Britons to donate instinctively at such sites their 'lucky scarves', favourite teddy bears, toys and other gifts in a way that is immediately reminiscent of the response made by our continental 'catholic' neighbours at Lourdes, Fatima and hundreds of lesser shrines across Europe. This is hardly an emotion wrought of ease of travel; rather it seems to be an instinctive sacramentalism.

Wesley Carr has called this whole phenomenon of institutional mourning 'sophisticated primitiveness' in which people move together in a state both of high dependency and loss to a further state of profound self-awareness. Yet they know what they are doing; it is not mass hysteria. This institutional mourning can be the means by which previously unresolved personal bereavement, going back not just a few months or even years, but for very long periods, can be expressed. Such unresolved grief, which has lain dormant in lives, having unknown effects, can, says Carr, be released by public grieving and enable some significant and psychological change to take place.

This modern perception, which is demonstrably held by a vast number of people in their need to provide shrines and ceremonies to which they can relate, contains a clear message to the Church. In this respect we are no longer always providing an adequate vehicle for the natural need to grieve and mourn. It is a challenge to which we must return.

Nevertheless, as the *Guidelines for Faith Communities* has emphasized, there will almost certainly be an expectation that a church service will be held. The *Guidelines* maintain that the purpose of any ceremony should be clearly defined from the outset. That helpful document also includes a timely warning that in organizing a service there may be difficulties between reconciling the needs of survivors, relatives of those who have died, and people who were involved in the rescue, with the attention which is attracted by visiting dignitaries. This is especially crucial when the presence of such people may involve high security arrangements which may seem to detract from the central purpose of the occasion. There is always a danger that these distractions can tempt us away from our duty to provide succour for those who most need our help.

Chapter 4

Planning the Service

It is the experience of those churches which have many memorial services that there is no substitute for an orderly series of planning meetings following a regular order and sequence. It would seem wise to give all services such care for detail: though granted not all services will need every part of the detailed planning described here. In some cases only one meeting may be necessary, at which all important points are covered. At each meeting a careful note should be kept of any decisions made. Much distress and annoyance can be thus avoided. This may seem unduly rigorist but experience has proved that it is the kindest and most pastorally sensitive approach. We must remember that it is almost certain some of the participants in these discussions will still be grieving and great sensitivity is required. Some decisions can be changed or modified, but many have to be made at an early stage. It is important to make it quite clear which they are, and final deadlines agreed and recorded.

PRELIMINARY MEETING

It will be at the first meeting, perhaps with merely one or more persons from each party involved, that some of these parameters will be explained. A cleric will preside. Almost certainly the following will be included:

The building
The size of the building and its seating capacity will strictly govern the number of those attending. Although in many cathedrals and churches there will be more than adequate space, in others it will be limited to a greater or lesser degree. The addition of chairs in aisles and passages is always to be discouraged, not least in these days of health, safety and fire precautions. Churches are only slowly beginning to realize their responsibilities in these matters. The matter of easy access and evacuation can be particularly important at these services. In some cases there will be a high proportion of more elderly participants, one of whom may suddenly be taken ill. Again at all these services the emotional level is bound to be high and can prove to be too much for some. In

both possible circumstances access with the least fuss and bother is needed to avoid embarrassment all round.

The service

It is essential at the earliest possible stage to explain that memorial services have no fixed liturgical form. There are models and resources, for instance those in *Common Worship: Pastoral Services* (pp. 331–401; this guide pp. 78–9) and others listed in this text, but they are not definitive. A number of decisions will need to be made, at the next stage, about music, hymns, readings and addresses.

In some cases the deceased has left a request, either formally or informally, for the inclusion of some item; this must be treated seriously, but ought not to bind 'the organizers' (for want of a better term). However, that does not mean that the organizers have carte blanche over the contents. Obviously the greatest possible sensitivity is required over this matter. All need to keep in mind the fact that it is a service in a Christian church conducted by a Christian minister despite any reservations some may have on religious matters. While avoiding any explicit reference to the clerical veto, for such it is, it is essential that all are clear from the outset: the Christian character of the building and the officiant are not in dispute. This established, much subsequent heartache can be avoided.

The clergy

Aligned to this the minister needs to explain any limits to the participation of other clergy that exist. If the minister intends, as they most probably do, to be the principal and presiding ecclesiastic that needs to be stated. No doubt a warm invitation will be issued to others across the ecumenical scene to attend and indeed participate, but sometimes it is mistakenly believed that other clergy can be imported at whim rather than by the goodwill and invitation of those responsible for the building in which the service is taking place.

Music

This is always a possible area for misunderstanding. An early explanation of local guidelines is pastorally essential. The extent and limit of musical resources need to be explained, and again any ruling that may exist over types of music. Where the resources are limited, an early warning against overambitious choices is important. The importation of musicians is always possible either by those requesting the service or on offer from the church. Again it is always necessary to point out any limitations on such an arrangement. Local musicians, correctly, guard jealously their rights in these matters.

Fees and expenses

These are matters which both sides may hesitate to raise, but they need an early airing. The musical provision may well, in many circumstances, prove to be one of the major components in the final bill. There is often a complete misunderstanding about musical fees, particularly in large churches and cathedrals; a failure to understand that in those places musicians are not salaried or at least only under contract for a limited number of statutory services. Therefore as professionals, or semi-professionals, they rely on fees for their livelihood and must not be presumed to be a gratuitous provision. Often equally misunderstood is the range of those fees. They must be capable of reflecting a reasonable proportion of a day's work, taking into consideration both rehearsal and the travelling time of a professional musician. Even in less well-provided-for establishments there will at least be one musician who needs reasonable remuneration and perhaps amateurs who ought to have some token reward. These sums together with church fees, charges for heating and lighting, need careful explanation together with the arrangements for printing the order of service.

The service sheet

The provision of a well-designed and printed service sheet (which sometimes even the clergy are tempted to think of as a 'programme') is essential. Not only is it needed for congregational participation, but it is an item which many will wish to take away with them as a memento of the service. Once again early assignment of responsibility in this matter is most helpful. It may be that the ecclesiastical side insists on using their well-versed printer or perhaps their own in-house facilities; if so that needs to be said at this stage. Should there be a willingness to allow other means to be used it must be emphasized that nothing ought to be put in hand until after the next meeting when precise details will be decided. Before final printing a proof *must* be cleared by the church and no further alterations permitted subsequently without joint agreement.

The next meeting

A final preliminary must be a reminder that at the next, more detailed, planning meeting suggestions for music, hymns and readings will be required, together with the names of any speakers or readers.

THE FULL PLANNING MEETING

With the early provision of such helpful preliminary advice it should now be possible to set up a more comprehensive meeting which can carefully plan all the details of the service.

In attendance would be, from the church side, if at all possible, the person in charge of the church's music and then in addition, depending upon the scale of the occasion and the church staff, representatives of those who will have an active role to perform on the day of the service or who will be engaged in its planning and preparation. The possibility of a part-time member of staff needing to be paid at least expenses for such attendance must not be lost sight of. It is always preferable to over-staff the meeting rather than have too few there. As wide a distribution of information as possible is always better than the risk of a black hole appearing in the arrangements. The 'other side', as it were, will usually be reassured by such attention to detail rather than be intimidated by it. The chairman will, of course, introduce members of the team and explain their area of responsibility.

While the outline which follows will serve for the greatest of national occasions it is perfectly capable of being applicable to every memorial service. Scaling down to less formal circumstances is easily done but the essential principles of collaboration by all parties and the collegiality of the local team are unchanging, whatever the size of the operation. Be it in a chapterhouse or over tea around the parsonage table each situation requires professionalism and co-operation. It is believed that a comprehensive aide-memoire will best serve this goal. Therefore, with permission, the template used at Westminster Abbey for services there, in St Margaret's and in the Chapel of St Mary Undercroft in the Palace of Westminster has been generally relied upon in this section.

An agenda for a planning meeting might contain the following items, with the chairman kindly, gently, but firmly restricting discussion to one item at a time.

Date and time

It is not unknown for confusion still to exist about these basic facts. Final confirmation prevents any confusion. The time of any service needs to be given careful thought and local conditions considered. People travelling a distance must be able easily to obtain food and drink before or after the service; transport must be available; parking possible – and so on.

Number expected

In the preliminary meeting the extent of the church's seating has been discussed, but an estimate of the probable number of those who may attend needs to be discussed at this point. Experience shows that this is a very imprecise science – but a reasonable estimate should be attempted. It will have an effect on many other later decisions.

Official representatives

The names and offices of any VIPs who are expected to attend need to be shared. It is essential at this point to ascertain their exact and preferred style. Arrangements to meet them on arrival must be made. They will normally be greeted by the principal minister of the host church, not by members of the family nor by an official of any sponsoring body. Naturally car parking arrangements will be made and facilities provided for any donning of robes or insignia and information regarding these arrangements must be communicated to those concerned. Dignitaries would then be conducted to a reserved seat, by whom and where according to local custom. These more detailed matters need not be discussed at the meeting in places where they are part and parcel of daily life, but where they are not they are points which must not be overlooked, otherwise unnecessary offence can easily be given. In cases where precedence is involved it will be necessary for any dignitaries to be given a precise time for arrival, to which their staff must be requested to follow strictly. An early arrival can be as disorganizing as a late one, in a tight programme.

Design of service sheet cover

Issues involved here are, in the first place, what the service is to be called. This decision has probably been pre-empted by the press announcements, but that need not be the final word on the matter. Although the generic title for the services we are considering is 'memorial services' that title is presently in less frequent use in the service for individuals. Finding greater favour is 'A Service of Thanksgiving for the Life and Work of X'. The desire for the use of this phrase is inevitably accompanied by the request that the service should contain elements of thanksgiving, rather than mourning, and commonly provoking the observation that such would have been what the deceased would have wanted.

In the case of services of memorial following tragedies, more time and thought will almost certainly be required to agree on a title which reflects the needs both of the immediate mourners and the general public.

To return to the arrangements concerning services for individuals, the family will need to confirm the name or names to be used on the cover, post-nominal letters, offices or titles, any crests or symbols to be incorporated; often it is thought, without any disrespect for the Christian faith, that a cross is 'too funereal' for inclusion on this cover. A small detail to be decided, is the matter of life dates, whether they are to be quoted as round years or in precise days, months and years.

Themes for the service

This is now the opportunity for the meeting to have a general discussion on the nature and style of the service, without going into the precise details of particular ingredients. As has been already mentioned, there is a regular and common request that in services for individuals there should be an element of thanksgiving. Naturally this will be considerably more muted, if present at all, in the other category of services we are considering. In a service subsequent upon a tragedy there will almost certainly still be many elements of grief and mourning which need to be expressed by both family and friends as well as by the wider public and which must be allowed expression.

Examples of possible theme elements, in the case of individuals, are: rural or environmental concerns; nautical interests; military or civic connections; national or international associations; scholastic and academic achievements; technical involvements – the list cannot attempt to be exhaustive. Many of these elements could prove to be difficult, or even impossible, to represent in the hymns, music or readings, but an early opportunity of airing this point should prevent the possibility of omission by default, which would be a pity.

In the post-tragedy type of service the opportunity for such an approach may well be more limited because almost certainly its nature, as we have just acknowledged, needs to be more cathartic and such emphases may not be the best means to ensure that.

Elements of the service

The notes provided with the outline orders for a memorial service in *Common Worship: Pastoral Services* include this important piece of initial guidance which must never be overlooked:

> Care should be taken to ensure that there is a clear president throughout, who introduces and concludes the service, and that a number of other speakers, musical items and non-biblical readings does not unbalance the service from its focus on the word of God, prayer and thanksgiving. (p. 334)

THE BEGINNING

It is a liturgical truism that too often the weakest points of any of our services, whatever type, shape or form, are their beginnings and their endings. We do not give sufficient careful thought to either the start or the finish of our acts of worship and memorial services are no exception to this critical generalization.

What is needed, as early as possible, is a bidding prayer which sets out the reason for the gathering. There is no set form for this prayer for which careful drafting and preparation is needed. It is a declaration on behalf of all present of the purpose that unites them. The prayer should be succinct, without being brief; couched in terms which are accessible without being trivial or trite; never patronizing nor sermonic; making no false claims. The bidding is not a welcome, being more significant than that. Without pre-empting any subsequent address, the bidding prayer provides a broad brush outline rather than detail. Always fully prepared down to the last comma, it must be read with dignity and conviction, almost certainly by the principal resident minister in his or her presidential role. This will be done from a lectern or pulpit or from in front of the high altar, whichever point affords the greatest visibility to the majority present.

Considering the care that will have gone into the drafting of this prayer, it must be ensured a pre-eminent place in the order of service. Should anything precede it? It has become traditional to have an entrance hymn the purpose of which is to cover the formal entrance of choir and clergy. This may be a necessary solution, but other ways are possible: they may, for example, enter to organ or other music. If it is desired to shorten the final entrance procession it is always possible to have other formal entrances which precede that containing the principal participants. Again it is often most effective to have the choir enter without a hymn and then sing a *short* introit which acts as a musical introduction to the bidding prayer, in turn leading into an opening hymn. This order of events avoids a gap after the bidding prayer while, say, a reader comes forward.

HYMNS

In these meetings the clergy need to maintain their position as professional leaders and planners of worship. Without insensitively steamrollering the ideas that emerge they must explain the function of hymns in worship. The service is not *Desert Island Discs* (or for the more ancient *These You Have Loved*), nor even *Songs of Praise*. The hymns must be integral to the shape and progression of the service. As with other elements of the service there need not be a knee-jerk reaction regarding the choice of hymns; there are no hymns which are obligatory. It must be acknowledged that it is a disturbing fact that the public's 'repertoire' of hymns is getting smaller and smaller. This is not helped by the substitution of songs and choruses in school assemblies chosen for popular appeal and alleged 'singability' rather than theological content or musical merit. Craven though this phenomenon is, it is being replicated in the music at many family services, further impoverishing worship by withdrawing knowledge of more traditional liturgical music and hymnody.

The meeting will need guidance on this matter and a careful explanation of the issues. The counter-argument will inevitably be that 'we must sing hymns that people know' and a balance between those hymns and the less familiar must be granted, but not at the expense of the inclusion of totally inappropriate items.

The first hymn needs to be a strong one from the 'well-known' category. The use of items more usually connected with funerals (e.g. 'Abide with me', 'The Lord is my Shepherd') should, if included at all, come later, with a final hymn which unambiguously expresses the Christian faith to which the building is consecrated.

There are both obvious and not so obvious pitfalls in the choice of hymnody. Let a few random examples serve as illustrations. The hymn 'Jerusalem' does not contain a strong and unambiguous expression of Christianity. Blake's hymn (with its fine, popular and most singable Parry tune) contains a tranche of the artist and poet's peculiar prejudices. One does not need to be a cynic to answer honestly the question in the first stanza 'No, those feet did not walk there'. Recently 'I vow to thee my country' has had a revival (triggered, as so often these fashions are, by a royal occasion – in this case the wedding of the Prince and Princess of Wales). The main thrust of that hymn is not simple patriotism but an aspiration to the joys of the heavenly country. The main thrust of the words is emphasized when the second verse commences 'There is another country . . .'. Sometimes it is wise to remind folk that in 'Dear Lord and Father of mankind' the second line is 'forgive our foolish ways'; that 'Mine eyes have seen the glory' includes impenetrable lines about Christ being born in the beauty of the lilies; and that 'All things bright and beautiful' is actually a children's hymn. How often do we gather rushes by the water: every day?

PSALMS

The inclusion of a psalm is increasingly problematic as the use of Anglican and Gregorian chant becomes more and more a rarity outside cathedrals and collegiate churches. In these establishments, and in other places where there is a strong choral tradition, it is always best to leave psalm-singing to the choir, during which the congregation can be seated. In other places, if a psalm is requested, it is always possible to use one of the many metrical psalms. This means that Psalm 100 can be sung as 'All people that on earth do dwell' or Psalms 149 and 150 as 'O praise ye the Lord'. There are many other examples. It can be that a psalm might be read as a lesson, despite the fact that liturgical purists insist that psalms are for singing.

ANTHEMS

Staying with the subject of music: In places where a choral tradition flourishes, there is often a request for an anthem as one of the possible building blocks of a service. Here is another area where public knowledge is often sadly limited and any musicians attending the meeting need to be ready delicately to guide and advise. Fashions come and go and what is currently at the top of the Classic FM hit-list may be the least suitable for this particular service; nor may it be performable by the available musical resources. A vocal double quartet cannot always be expected to perform 'Zadok the priest', for example. The settings of *Panis Angelicus* are beautiful but we need to remember that it is about the Eucharist and may fail to resonate with a largely 'non-worshipping' congregation. If it is no more than a musical interlude then its inclusion is possible, but if each item is intended to contribute to a coherent whole, then a better choice is possible. The musicians should be prepared to suggest suitable alternatives from their repertoire.

A WORD OF WARNING

A note of warning about the inclusion in any service of the musical offerings of family friends or colleagues. Such offers should always be approached with extreme caution. In churches where there is a tradition of high musical excellence the inclusion of outside musicians, however well-intentioned, may contrast adversely with the resident choir, to the disadvantage of the visitors. It is not always easy for the congregation to distinguish the various groups, a fact which may, rightly or wrongly, be resented by a proficient choir rehearsing hard to maintain its standards. This also applies to the intrusion of a visiting organist, perhaps unfamiliar with the instrument. The size, compass and tonal colours of the instrument will be best known to the regular organist. Visiting musicians even when technically accomplished may well be unused to accompanying the singing of a large congregation or of a small vocal group. None of these points are suggested as absolute rules, and each has the possibility of many exceptions; this warning is intended to forearm those charged with planning. What at the time may be a kind and generous decision, made perhaps on sentimental grounds, may be much regretted on the day of the service. Further it is the duty of the clergy to draw attention to the highly charged nature of these occasions which often evoke emotional problems for even the most experienced performer. It serves neither the occasion nor the performer to risk any possibility of such distressing consequences.

A study of the appropriate pages of the broadsheet newspapers reveals an increasing tendency to include secular music in memorial services; often by a small ensemble or a solo instrument (sometimes even the organ). This is usually widely appreciated and provides a useful time for reflection. This music need not be avowedly religious yet there are limits and discretion is imperative. While jazz bands and 'songs from the shows' may just be appropriate at St Paul's, Covent Garden to say farewell to show-business personalities, they will almost certainly strike a false note elsewhere. 'He loved jazz' is not always sufficient justification for its inclusion in a church service. If incorporated at all the possibility is that it can be used at the conclusion. That it is not, however, the time at which to play one's trump card, if this is how it is perceived. We shall return to this later. Equally favourite songs ('our tune') will only rarely provide added value to the kind of service under consideration. While it is true that crematoria report Frank Sinatra's 'My way' as among the most popular choices of recorded music at cremations, we ought to do better than that in any church service. At any rate that particular song is so obviously a denial of any form of divine guidance or of the absolute necessity of our need of God's grace during our earthly pilgrimage. Throughout a religious service the necessity for truth remains mandatory.

READINGS

It is as well to have some previously decided principle regarding readings at memorial services which can be explained at an early stage. Whatever else is included, there must be one reading from the New Testament. This then allows scope for the inclusion of poems, literary extracts and such like. Additionally, it may be felt that there is sufficient wisdom literature in the Bible without having to resort to the writings of the religious writer inaccurately known as the 'Prophet', Kahlil Gibran.

Having become unduly lax in the standard of reading performance in our ordinary church services, we may be under some difficulty in insisting that readers be chosen on the sole ground of the ability to read well on a public occasion. Their role of representative of this or that (including the family) at a service for an individual should not be regarded as sufficient justification to be uncritically allotted this important task. Organizations are not likely to suggest the name of a competent (but junior) reader over against a managing director, especially if it is known that each week the church entrusts the proclamation of sacred scripture to a brownie guide or cub scout or a semi-inaudible parishioner without a thought about the dignity of the word of God in divine worship.

It is essential that all non-scriptural readings are vetted. They must be suitable for reading in church and not contain any passages which are antipathetic to the Christian faith. A certain amount of reverent agnosticism may perhaps be allowed. This emerges in some poetry. It may, for example, be asserted that Dylan Thomas' 'Do not go gentle into that good night', is no more agnostic regarding the risen life than many possible choices from the Old Testament.

Some non-scriptural readings have become hackneyed without necessarily being the best examples of the genre. The most obvious example is Canon Henry Scott Holland's passage 'Death is nothing at all'. In the starkness of this much used fragment of a sermon preached in St Paul's Cathedral a few days after the death of King Edward VII, there is little of a full comprehension of the Christian attitude to death. Death *is* indeed a very real thing, which can devastate families, communities and individuals. Henry Scott Holland actually deals with some of these issues in that sermon ('How black, how relentless, this total lack of tangible evidence for the certainty we believe in!' he says) and the full text is completely orthodox, which is more than can be said for the normally used extract. Of that an American has commented that the message comes across as 'I'm not dead; I'm just on hold'. One wonders how often Scott Holland would be wheeled out by some, if his Christian Socialist convictions were more widely recalled.

Poetry, though a popular choice, does add an additional hurdle for prospective readers. Prose needs careful preparation and rehearsal – poetry requires an extra skill which those who are otherwise good readers may not necessarily possess. Even some actors shy away from reading verse. The efforts required to raise the reader of prose to an acceptable standard of proficiency are at best nothing to those required for poetry. An incompetent reading of poetry can render it entirely incomprehensible. A rehearsal, in church, is essential for all readers; those tackling poetry, it must be agreed, may need to accept extensive coaching in order that their contribution might be intelligible to the hearers.

There is the very mixed blessing of the now ubiquitous microphone! Experienced public speakers will have been trained in microphone technique which includes an inviolable rule to check out all systems beforehand. Each one differs and the acoustic of every building is quite unique. Those who have not acquired these skills must be offered carefully nuanced help.

Depending upon the structure of the service it may be that two of the readings occur 'back to back'. In this case the two readers should be encouraged to come forward together, going either to different positions (pulpit or lectern) or one directly to the reading position with the other waiting nearby and then swapping positions before returning to their seats together. This avoids a hiatus during which the congregation awaits the next reading. Although there are some musical items which can be ruined by being used as a covering for movement, and musicians rightly deplore such musical insensitivity, further gaps can be avoided if adequate time is allowed for readers to leave their seats during a hymn, psalm or anthem, and be ready at its conclusion. The only pause should be that which enables the congregation to settle and refocus their attention. All that remains is for readers to be given clear instructions on how to begin and end. Biblical readings can conclude in one of the traditional ways: 'Here ends the lesson' or 'Thanks be to God', whereas non-scriptural readings do not need any such appendages, in fact they are often diminished by such an addition. The only necessity in such cases is a suitable pause. Readings do not need to be printed out in full on the service sheet. Listening to the readings should be a shared experience for the whole congregation.

Occasionally there is a particularly appropriate piece of prose or poetry which proves difficult to fit into the service; it is perhaps a little too personal. The problem can be solved by printing the passage in the service sheet where it can be read by members of the congregation before or after the service. There is an example of this in the service for Eric Heffer on page 41.

ADDRESS (OR ADDRESSES)
In the case of services commemorating individuals the present fashion seems to favour the plural. Sometimes there is an attempt to differentiate between types of addresses by stating that some of them are 'giving tribute'. These are intended to be brief and attempt, where the person's life contained a variety of aspects, to deal with each sufficiently. The word 'sermon' seems entirely to have disappeared from the modern memorial service for individuals. The vast majority of speakers are lay people who would have an immediate horror at the prospect of preaching. It seems a pity that the clergy have largely abrogated their responsibilities in this matter as far as memorial services are concerned. These are large gatherings of folk in our churches. A sermon, containing the living hope of the gospel, which was not over long and did not seem to be taking advantage of a captive audience, might be more welcome than we might seem to imagine.

Further, we may be certain, that if there is no such sermon, there will only be panegyrics. One astute observer of the present-day scene sums them up: they describe 'an unblemished life of seamless virtue, blessed by good temper, humour and the unmitigated admiration of friends and foe'. Perhaps it is too late and impossible to stem the flow of such sentiments; despite the fact that we are no longer *burying* Caesar, we can do no other than praise him it would seem.

It is the duty of those planning such services to ensure that the address (or addresses) do not skew the balance. This is likely to occur unless special guidance is given to speakers concerning the length of these contributions. It has been found that advice is more helpfully afforded by pointing out that 1,000 words can be delivered in ten minutes. In an hour-long service, surely the maximum length for any such occasion, the allocation for addresses would probably between 15 and 20 minutes giving the possibility of 1,500–2,000 words of script. This will need to be divided in an agreed way if there is more than one speaker.

As for addresses at services following a disaster, this matter should almost invariably be in the hands of the clergy. It ought to be otiose to say that such preaching will need the most careful and prayerful preparation. This is certainly one occasion when another eye cast over the script would be invaluable: too rare a custom for the present-day clergy, I fear. Unintentional insensitivities can thus be avoided. In these circumstances it will also be necessary to speak from a full script in order that families and friends may have a copy, if they so wish. The media should, when necessary, be provided with a copy to ensure accurate quotation; indeed an embargoed press release may be advisable, prepared with the advice and expertise of a Diocesan Press Office, or other central body.

PRAYERS

The choice of the prayers to be used at either type of memorial service is mainly the responsibility of the clergy. However, themes and ideas suggested by the mourners should always be taken into consideration and inform the contents of the prayers.

Litany type intercessions are difficult to make work with a largely non-church-going congregation, and should be used with caution. This is despite the fact that such a method is often the most elegant way of incorporating details not usually the subject of our prayers. As should always be the case, care must be taken to ensure that all intercession is directed to the first person of the Trinity, through the Son and in the power of the Spirit. Equally any prayer should not seem to be imparting information to the Almighty, nor be overspecific as to the response we believe might best flow from God's mercy. Nonetheless, while retaining a certain objectivity, the prayers should not be so general, or so anodyne, that they provide neither comfort nor inspiration to participants.

The use of a moment of corporate recollection, as a preliminary to, or conclusion of, the prayer section is often appreciated. A brief exhortation such as 'In silence before God, let us remember N with thanksgiving' or 'Let us each in silence bring before God our own memories of N' may be employed. After a brief silence the first of the prayers can be said. In services which follow a tragedy the slow reading of a list of names can be very moving. The reader will, of course, have checked (and double-checked) all pronunciations.

The use of a minimum of 'formal' prayers is advisable. Prayers such as those of St Ignatius Loyola ('Teach us, good Lord'), Sir Jacob Ashley before Edgehill ('Thou knowest how busy I must be this day') or even Reinhold Niebuhr's 'serenity prayer' ('serenity to accept the things I cannot change; courage to change the things I can . . .') unfortunately too often appear to be emblematic rather than devotional. A similar effect may be produced by the so-called Prayer of St Francis ('Make us instruments of thy peace'). This prayer, which is in fact a nineteenth-century French composition of unknown authorship, owes nothing to the pen of Francis of Assisi and suffers badly from overuse.

The inclusion of classical prayers alongside more contemporary compositions will raise the question of whether 'you and yours' prayers can be used in close juxtaposition with those couched in hierarchical language. Many feel that 'thee and thou' prayers can be used alongside modern forms as long as both are of high quality. Ronald Jasper, the main architect of the *Alternative Service Book*, maintained that just as modern and period architecture can co-exist in the same street if they are both of high quality, so can good prayers from different periods. Crude Tudor pastiche can be as offensive to the ear as both informal chatty prayers interspersed with the inevitable adverb 'just', and infelicitously constructed avant-garde orisons. Some of Eric Milner White's original compositions, once thought to be superb models of a modern collect form, are now almost unusable.

Another contemporary concern surrounds the use of 'inclusive language'. Liturgical texts for funeral services have always been sensitive to this: the Prayer Book, for instance, italicizes 'brother' throughout in the service for the Burial of the Dead. Those drafting or choosing prayers for present-day services need to be cautious, particularly when the service is for a woman or, in the case of services in tragic circumstances, where the victims are both women and men. Many traditional prayers are very male-oriented and their inclusion could seem to be tactless.

It is important to remember that the Anglican tradition of a series of prayers in the style of 'after the third collect', is practically unknown in Free Church and Roman Catholic worship. This means that in a memorial service which is being shared ecumenically this part of the service may need to be explained to non-Anglican participants and guidance given; not least the point of the ascription at the end of each prayer with its anticipation of a congregational 'amen'.

All would agree that the Lord's Prayer is an essential ingredient in the prayers, probably as one of the final items in the main prayer section. It may well be prefaced by some such phrase as 'we sum up all these our prayers with the words our Saviour taught us'. In services in which the congregation is drawn mainly from one church the form of the Lord's Prayer used can be that which is normal at any other service in that place. However in cases where people have come from many different

places and traditions what is known as the modified traditional (and ecumenically agreed) form ('Our Father, who art') must always be used.
Nevertheless it is a courtesy to print the text in full in the service sheet
to avoid confusion.

The conclusion of this part of the service can be by using the Grace (2
Corinthians 13.14) perhaps said by all. There are other such brief concluding prayers (see References) which are appropriate. If the Pauline
'Grace' is to be used congregationally that too should be printed in full
to avoid any confusion.

THE END OF THE SERVICE
It has already been asserted that there should be a strong hymn at the end
of the service which resonates with the Christian context in which it has
been held irrespective of the faith of those commemorated or the individual beliefs of the congregation. 'Thine be the glory', which in recent
years has become widely known, is an obvious candidate, as is 'Who
would true valour see' (in a version avoiding the male pronoun) – but
there are many other possibilities.

A monetary collection at this point is intrusive. Support for a favourite charity is best taken at an early stage or even better left to a retiring
collection with this fact flagged in the service sheet.

The service sheet could also clearly state that the congregation should
remain standing at the end of the hymn. This obviates a double rising
and kneeling over a very short period when a hymn is followed by a
short prayer and a blessing. This short prayer should recapitulate the
overall purpose of the service. For an individual, perhaps a final act of
thanksgiving; in the case of a disaster the needs of the distressed must
be included. The blessing can take any of the traditional forms. In an ecumenical service this can be graciously shared among other participants
at the invitation of the minister, having provided a full text of the blessing for the benefit of such colleagues.

After the blessing the organist should provide a stirring voluntary.
This is preferable to other instrumental music (except perhaps a military
or brass band) as the level of noise created by a departing congregation
usually drowns any subtle or delicate sounds. Certainly choral music
rarely works at this point. It is an occasion for the organist's talents to
be displayed; sadly they must also be ignored. In other words, it is inad-
visable to put any particular precious or significant eggs into this
basket. They will not generally be heard or appreciated.

Other decisions
There are other matters of greater or lesser importance which require
agreed decisions at the planning meeting. Flowers are an almost

obligatory ingredient and need a few minutes' thought – who provides, who arranges, where are they permitted, where are they seen at their best in the church? There is also the question of the not inconsiderable cost both of flowers and their arrangements.

Sometimes a custom or added ceremonial will visually personalize the service. This might include the processing of medals and decorations carefully secured on to a cushion and borne by grandchildren, family or colleagues; the carrying of symbols of office – chains, badges, wands or staves and other insignia. Sporting equipment, a cricket bat, a football have been used in this way. In this care should be taken that any such ceremony should not seem jejune or immodest. The character of the one being commemorated needs to be kept clearly in mind before any final decision is made.

Additional administrative matters

The amount of time to be spent at the planning meeting over administrative matters will vary enormously according to the size, complexity and significance (local, regionally or nationally) of the occasion. However, even the smallest service deserves an attention to detail which will avoid all unnecessary distress or embarrassment. The wise planner will know which of the following matters apply in any particular circumstances.

PRESS NOTICES

The importance of these has been alluded to earlier. A decision as to which national or local newspapers are to be used must be made. The details in the notice should be clear and precise – and always carefully checked with those concerned. In some cases the notice will, in particular, make clear whether or not those attending need to notify anyone of their intention to attend. Such notification does not necessarily imply that tickets will be issued. It may only be necessary to give an indication of numbers. These distinctions between a tickets-only occasion and notification occasion need to be clear. If there are no tickets but a need to inform the organizers some such formula as 'all welcome, no tickets required, but notification of an intention to attend would be appreciated' is advisable in press notices.

TICKETS

If tickets are thought necessary, directions for making application must be given in the press notice together with an indication as to when they will be dispatched. This relieves (but sadly does not totally remove) administrators of the harassment of overanxious members of the public making enquiries before tickets have been issued. Colour coding tickets for large affairs is of greatest help to stewards at the service. Making the prior decisions which this involves goes a considerable way towards avoiding awkward problems of precedence and protocol. The ticket will include a direction as to the latest time for the congregation to be seated. This stipulation will have taken into consideration sufficient time for the arrival and reception of families, any VIPs or special guests.

STEWARDS

Most churches have their own team of stewards or sidespersons, but they may well appreciate additional help if the service is likely to attract large numbers. The presiding minister will be sensitive to any risk of toe-treading in this area and would advise on the details of such planning. There is one particular area in which assistance is usually appreciated – the identification of particularly close family and friends. This task is best entrusted to a member (or members) of such categories. It may be kind to assemble the closest members of the bereaved family or families in a suitable place on their own ahead of the service and then have them taken directly to their seats in church. Mingling with friends after the service is supportive and always appreciated; before the service it can be seen as an intrusion.

FIRST AID

In large gatherings it is always advisable to have obtained the services of St John's Ambulance Brigade or the Red Cross. The emotion of such occasions can prove too much for some; prior precautions are better than having to resort to an embarrassing 'Is there a doctor in the house?' emergency call.

DRESS

We live in increasingly casual days and the incidence of formal dress occasions is now rare. Yet there are circumstances, in some places, in which guidance will be needed about men's dress (most women have an unerring ability to know instinctively what they ought to wear). In some churches memorial services remain (with weddings) the only time a morning coat is worn. Principal mourners, VIPs and stewards need forewarning if this now less frequent form of dress is to be worn.

MEDIA ARRANGEMENTS

In high-profile circumstances it is impossible not to be overscrupulous in checking and then rechecking the arrangements for the media. The importance of providing a full text of any addresses has already been mentioned and the advisability of obtaining professional support when media interest is high. If photographs or TV coverage is anticipated the principal mourners need to be informed. It may be that they do not wish this to happen, in which case their views need to be taken into consideration. Sometimes on 'national' occasions they will need to be persuaded that a limited and controlled 'photo opportunity' is preferable to an unseemly free for all. Such opportunities would be provided after (occasionally before) the service, outside the church building, perhaps in a porch or narthex. TV coverage and photographs within the church are always under the strict control of the appropriate ecclesiastical authorities, so there should be no problems on that front. Even so any church-issued permissions to film or photograph need to have been the subject of liaison both with the intimate members of the family and probably the appropriate representative of any very senior VIPs (e.g. royalty).

AUDIO/VIDEO RECORDINGS

As has been stated, any coverage of the service, by any means, is precisely controlled by ecclesiastical rules. Any requests for such recordings need to be made at an early stage, and placed in the hands of an experienced operator. Strict criteria must be agreed. A wandering hand-held video camera can be completely disruptive in a service. Set, agreed positions should be insisted upon. Equally insistence on the use of an experienced operator ought to preclude the engagement of a well-meaning friend rather than a professional or semi-professional, whose equipment and technique is unequal to particularly the light challenges of church interiors and the limited available camera angles. Similar difficulties will be avoided by engaging an expert sound engineer. A multitude of microphones is essential if anything like a reasonable recording is to be made. Those who have seen a church wired for sound before a BBC broadcast will appreciate the need for a highly technical and well-equipped system. Merely plugging into the church's public address system will not produce a satisfactory result – almost certainly all congregational and choral contributions will be absent. If music is to be included on any audio/video tape negotiations will be necessary if any professional musicians are involved; extra fees are payable. The matter of copyright should not be overlooked. There is the possibility that the service contains words (including readings) and music for which a copyright fee is payable.

Conclusion

Supplied with all this information the task remains for the presiding minister to take the various suggestions, requests, half-thought-out ideas that have emerged and shape them into a service.

This may involve one or two drafts, in order to ensure that the service has momentum and dignity, does justice to the departed and provides consolation and hope for the bereaved. It must never be forgotten that it is a Christian service whatever hesitations any of the participants might have about Christianity. The minister's abiding responsibility is to guarantee that the Christian faith is certainly implicit in the details of the service and, overall, is sensitively explicit.

Chapter 5

A Critical Overview by Some Practitioners

The responsibility for the final ordering of any memorial service, as has been stated at the end of the last chapter, lies with the senior pastor; be that dean, incumbent or minister. It is they who must use experience and informed perception to ensure that what has been agreed finds liturgical expression. Memorial services, in common with all worship, are to the greater glory of God, not to the greater glory of the commemorated.

This is not easily achieved. It was one of the concerns expressed in a series of consultations held in the early 1990s between the then Dean of Westminster (Michael Mayne), Canon Geoffrey Brown (Vicar of St Martin-in-the-Fields 1985–95) and myself. At the time, all three of us were deeply involved in the planning, preparation and celebration of many memorial services at the Abbey, St Margaret's Westminster Abbey and St Martin-in-the-Fields. Each brought a variety of experience to our discussions garnered from earlier experience at Great St Mary's, Cambridge, Grimsby Parish Church and Liverpool Parish Church.

As a group of practitioners we were agreed that with the waning of conventional religious practice and an ambiguity towards doctrines formerly universally accepted, the focus of attention in any funereal rite has changed. No longer is attention mainly given to the themes of judgement, forgiveness and eternal life: the soul's relation to God is no longer the main consideration. Instead the central concern is the person who has died and a desire to give expression to the character of the deceased, their history and relationships.

In consequence many contemporary memorial services are simply a celebration of a life. Although Christian hymns are sung, Christian prayers are said, and passages from holy scripture read, these are no longer the heartland of the ceremony. For the vast majority of the congregation at the centre stands the tributes, the sharing of memories, the recalling of achievements. It is as if through these reflections the dead person, for one glorious moment, might be made alive.

In a paper submitted to the group Geoffrey Brown suggested,

> I believe that the modern phenomenon of the memorial service is a direct result of the decline in conventional religious belief. There is a deep instinct and need to deny the finality of death, and yet there is little doctrinal faith

to sustain a conventional Christian hope – and this kind of ignorance is likely to grow just so long as the number of those receiving basic Christian teaching remains comparatively small.

The group was agreed in welcoming many aspects of the renewed celebration of life and goodness which occur in many contemporary services in this genre: and the proper recognition of all that is good, loving and beautiful reflects the nature of God. Equally noteworthy is that in spite of the increasing popularity of entirely secular memorial meetings, most people still seek us out. They identify the Church as the proper place for the celebration of a life and for an engagement with the questions of death.

We were also of one mind in agreeing that the problem with many contemporary memorial services from the Christian point of view is that they too easily degenerate into mere cheerful sentimentality or total dishonesty. As a result they fail to address the deep and serious issue that life is a gift from God and that we are not just accountable to our friends and admirers, or even to the rest of the human race, but to God himself. Only God can truly exercise his loving mercy to any of us and then only if we are willing to admit to the bad as well as the good in all human affairs.

In one of his contributions to a discussion on the form and content of a memorial service, Michael Mayne explained,

> I try to encourage the family to consider what they are really wanting the service to say and to choose hymns, readings and music which will a) not be too hackneyed, and b) express the personality of the departed within a context of thanksgiving, celebration and (less easily achieved) penitence.

Dean Mayne found us in full agreement that this policy too often falls down when we fail to find the right passages from scriptures or elsewhere for a particular person. So often the hackneyed passage is asked for and accepted, simply because it is easier and time-saving. This raises the whole question of meeting people's expressed (but often immature) needs and expectations. It challenges us to find the resources, skill and time to suggest new and appropriate words to fit each particular occasion.

We were all agreed that memorial services provide enormous opportunities for the Church and that many services about which we had initial hesitations, to our surprise proved to be very 'spiritual' occasions. This is worthwhile ministry for the Church and we ought not to be mealy-mouthed or patronizing about these services. They deserve the careful planning which this guide has described and should be afforded the highest degree of pastoral and liturgical care.

Chapter 6

Exemplars

INTRODUCTION

Four services which have taken place in recent years have been included in this chapter. They are not intended for slavish imitation, but as examples of ways in which well-known material can be blended together with that which is not as familiar in order to produce what always must be a unique service for each occasion. The sample services for individuals are those which were held for two well-known public figures. These examples were chosen in order that the relevance of the contents of the service can be examined. Similarly the two other services were produced in the wake of profound and widespread public shock which can still be easily recalled. Perfection is not claimed for any of these services, but each was prepared in the belief that maximum sensitivity had been applied to their planning.

Each of these services was unique, designed for a particular individual or in especially tragic circumstances. The material was judged to be appropriate, nothing was included as a matter of course. A similar care for detail ought to characterize all memorial services.

The abbreviations used in the orders of service are:
NEH   New English Hymnal
AMNS   Ancient and Modern New Standard
CP   Common Praise

SERVICE FOR ERIC HEFFER MP

Eric Heffer was one of the best-known parliamentarians of his time. An uncompromising socialist who was also one of the great rebels of twentieth-century British politics, he called his autobiography *Never a Yes Man*. Towards the end of that book, written in the last months of his life, he says 'For me . . . my socialism and my Christianity have become even more intertwined. In working for a classless society without poverty for the many on the one hand and riches for the few on the other, I have worked for God's Kingdom here on earth.' When designing the service sheet the opportunity was taken to reproduce quotations from Heffer's book *Why I Am a Christian*, which was due to be published posthumously some weeks after the service. This was thought to be more suitable than including extracts as readings in the service.

The bidding prayer, written with the assistance of his family, emphasizes Heffer's political aspirations as well as his recognition of his Lord both in the hungry and homeless and in the Blessed Sacrament to which he had great devotion.

The first hymn was by the Christian Socialist Canon of St Paul's, Henry Scott Holland. The Speaker of the House of Commons read the passage known as 'the Golden Rule' from the Sermon on the Mount. Sandwiched between the addresses was a little-known hymn (to a well-known tune). This hymn by another socialist, the artist, craftsman and poet William Morris, was sung at the funeral of one of Heffer's heroes Fr Conrad Noel. 'Over the years the teachings of priests like Conrad Noel had a strong influence on me,' Eric Heffer wrote.

The Elgar setting of *Ave Verum Corpus* was chosen, not merely for its musical beauty, but because of Eric Heffer's perhaps not well-known, yet deeply held, devotion to the Blessed Sacrament. He regularly and deliberately prayed in Westminster Abbey's St George's Chapel where the Blessed Sacrament was at that time reserved. This point was made in a brief address after the motet and before two prayers: the first of which speaks of the Church as the extension of the incarnation and the second was the collect for the Feast of Corpus Christi.

'Jerusalem' was the final hymn. For many years it has been sung at Labour rallies and Christian Socialist meetings.

St Margaret's Church
Westminster Abbey

A Service of Thanksgiving for the Life and Work of Eric Samuel Heffer MP
1922–1991

Wednesday 10 July 1991

For years, as a Communist, then as a Socialist, I did not believe, or thought I did not. Then I went to Israel in 1968 and visited the Church of the Holy Sepulchre. I walked along the Via Dolorosa almost as in a trance. Here was the path that Christ had trodden, persecuted every inch of the way. The crown of thorns, the Cross became real. I could see in my mind's eye the agony of Christ, the suffering he carried for the poor. He was to be crucified because of his love for them. The people who watched this – some, as always, mistakenly glad; others, suffering with Christ every inch of his painful path. I could see it all. It was as if I was at the crucifixion itself, and all my early beliefs came flooding back. I felt bathed in a bright light, and Christ was saying to me, 'Come with me, we are on the same side. I fought in my day for what you believe in to-day. I am the son of God, you must help to secure God's kingdom'.

Why I did not proclaim my experience from the house-tops, I'm not really sure, except that because I was an MP I feared I would not be believed, and there would be those who would accuse me of looking for publicity or pulling some kind of political stunt.

Eric S. Heffer, *Why I Am a Christian*
(to be published in September 1991)

ORDER OF SERVICE

All stand as The Speaker of the House of Commons is received at the East Door by the Rector of St Margaret's and conducted to his place.

After the Choir and Clergy have taken their places, the Reverend Dr Donald Gray, Canon of Westminster and Chaplain to the Speaker of the House of Commons, says

THE BIDDING

We are gathered as family and friends to give thanks to Almighty God for the life and work of Eric Samuel Heffer,

Trade Unionist,
Parliamentarian,
Christian Socialist,
Husband and Friend.

We remember with thanksgiving his zest for life, his courage, and his kindliness.

In a life dedicated to the poor and underprivileged, he devoted himself to their needs and aspirations, working ceaselessly for the advancement of their opportunities and for greater fulfilment in their lives.

As he laboured for the establishment of the kingdom of God on earth, Eric was not oblivious to the claims of the kingdom of Heaven. So he prepared himself carefully and bravely to give his account to the God he served, by trusting in the power of the Cross and Resurrection of Jesus Christ.

'Lord, when was it that we saw you hungry and fed you, or thirsty and gave you drink, a stranger and took you home, or naked and clothed you? When did we see you ill or in prison, and come and visit you?'

'I tell you this: anything you did for one of my brothers here, however humble, you did for me.'

Eric recognised his Lord both in Sacrament and in service and so made ready to meet the Judge eternal.

All remain standing to sing

HYMN

Judge eternal, throned in splendour
NEH 490; CP 356

All sit for

THE LESSON

read by the Right Honourable Bernard Weatherill MP
Speaker of the House of Commons
St Mark 12.28–34

One of the lawyers, who had been listening to these discussions and had noted how well Jesus answered, came forward and asked him, 'Which commandment is first of all?' Jesus answered, 'The first is, "Hear, O Israel: the Lord our God is the only Lord; love the Lord your God with all your heart, with all your soul, with all your mind, and with all your strength." The second is this: "Love your neighbour as yourself." There is no other commandment greater than these.' The lawyer said to him, 'Well said, Master. You are right in saying that God is one and beside him there is no other. And to love him with all your heart, all your understanding, and all your strength, and to love your neighbour as yourself – that is far more than any burnt offerings or sacrifices.' When Jesus saw how sensibly he answered, he said to him, 'You are not far from the kingdom of God.'

All stand to sing

PSALM 146.1, 5–10

All sit for

AN ADDRESS

given by Ian Aitken
Political Columnist, The Guardian

All stand to sing

HYMN

Hear a word, a word in season,
For the day is drawing nigh,
When the Cause shall call upon us,
Some to live, and some to die!
He that dies shall not die lonely,
Many an one hath gone before;
He that lives shall bear no burden
Heavier than the life they bore.

Some had name, and fame, and honour,
Learn'd they were, and wise and strong;
Some were nameless, poor, unlettered,
Weak in all but grief and wrong.
Named and nameless all live in us;
One and all they lead us yet
Every pain to count for nothing,
Every sorrow to forget.

Life or death then, who shall heed it,
What we gain or what we lose?
Fair flies life amid the struggle,
And the Cause for each shall choose.
Hear a word, a word in season,
For the day is drawing nigh,
When the Cause shall call upon us,
Some to live, and some to die!

Ludwig van Beethoven, 1770–1827
Tune from last movement of
Symphony IX

William Morris, 1834–96
from a poem
'All for the Cause'

All sit for

ADDRESSES

given by Sir Robert Rhodes James MP
and
the Right Honourable Tony Benn MP

All remain seated while the Choir sing

THE ANTHEM

Ave verum corpus, natum ex Maria Virgine
Vere passum immolatum in cruce pro homine.
Cujus latus perforatum vero fluxit sanguine.
Esto nobis praegustatum mortis in examine,
O clemens, O pie, O dulcis Jesu, Fili Mariae.

> *Jesu, Word of God Incarnate,*
> *Of the Virgin Mary born,*
> *On the Cross Thy sacred Body*
> *For us men with nails was torn.*
> *Cleanse us, by the blood and water*
> *Streaming from thy pierced side,*
> *Feed us with thy Body broken,*
> *Now, and in death's agony:*
> *O Jesu, hear us, Son of Mary.*

Ave verum corpus   *Edward Elgar, 1857–1934*
Anon 14th Century

After a brief

INTRODUCTION

given by Canon Gray, all kneel for

THE PRAYERS

Christ has no Body now on earth but yours,
No hands but yours,
No feet but yours;
Yours are the eyes through
  which is to look on Christ's
  compassion to the world;
Yours are the feet with which
  he is to go about doing good;
Yours are the hands with which
  he is to bless men now.

St Teresa of Avila, 1515–82

A Thanksgiving for the Holy Eucharist:

> Almighty and heavenly Father,
> We thank you that in this wonderful sacrament
> You have given us the memorial
> Of the passion of your Son Jesus Christ.
> Grant us so to reverence
> The sacred mysteries of his body and blood,
> That we may know within ourselves
> And show forth in our lives the fruits of his redemption;
> Who is alive and reigns with you and the Holy Spirit,
> One God, now and for ever. *Amen.*

> *St Thomas Aquinas, c1225–74*
> *Collect for the Feast of Corpus Christi*

The Reverend Nicholas Frayling, Rector of Liverpool, continues

A prayer for Eric:
Almighty Father: We bless your name for all who have completed their earthly course and are now at rest. We remember before you this day your servant, Eric, rendering thanks to you for the gift of his friendship, and for his life of service and devotion. In your loving wisdom and almighty power, work in him, as in us, all the good purpose of your holy will, through Jesus Christ our Lord. *Amen.*

A prayer for the Parliament he served:
O Lord, God of righteousness and truth, grant to our Queen and her Government, to Members of Parliament and all in positions of responsibility, the guidance of your Spirit. May they never lead the nation wrongly through love of power, desire to please, or unworthy ideals, but always love righteousness and truth; so may your kingdom be advanced and your name hallowed; through Jesus Christ our Lord. *Amen.*

We sum up all our prayers and petitions in the words our Lord Jesus Christ taught us, saying together:
Our Father, who art in heaven, hallowed be thy name; thy kingdom come; thy will be done; on earth as it is in heaven. Give us this day our daily bread. And forgive us our trespasses, as we forgive those who trespass against us. And lead us not into temptation; but deliver us from evil, for thine is the kingdom, the power and the glory, for ever and ever. Amen.

All stand to sing

HYMN

And did those feet in ancient time
NEH 488; AMNS 294; CP 356

All kneel for

A prayer for Doris and all those who mourn:

> Gracious Father,
> In darkness and in light,
> In trouble and in joy,
> Help us to trust your love,
> to serve your purpose, and
> to praise your name;
> Through Jesus Christ our Lord. *Amen*

and

THE BLESSING

God, who through the resurrection of our Lord Jesus Christ has given us the victory, give you joy and peace in your faith; and the blessing of God almighty, the Father, the Son and the Holy Spirit rest upon you and remain with you always. *Amen.*

SERVICE FOR THE RT REVD AND RT HON.
THE LORD RUNCIE

Lady Runcie has said, 'He chose his own funeral service, and we did the memorial one. I hope he was pleased with it too.' Certainly a great deal of trouble went into getting his memorial service right, so we may presume that Robert Runcie was well satisfied with the joint efforts of his family and the Dean and Chapter of Westminster. The funeral had been held at St Alban's Abbey, but this service needed to be in London and where better than Westminster Abbey in which Lord Runcie had been consecrated bishop 30 years earlier on 24 February 1970? The Abbey service was a great gathering of the distinguished and famous, led by the Prince of Wales, together with those who only knew of Robert Runcie from a distance as bishop or primate. As the bidding prayer said, the rich variety of life represented in the congregation witnessed to a singular man: Robert, 'archbishop and friend' who revelled in curiosity about the world – its history and its culture – and who courageously stood for the abiding values of Christianity. The prayer led into the singing of 'Come down, O Love divine' sung to the tune Vaughan Williams named after his father's Gloucestershire parish – Down Ampney. The hymn contains the words: 'Let holy charity mine outward vesture be, and lowliness become my inner clothing.'

Bishop Runcie's daughter read from the epistle to the Philippians and the Abbey choir sang Walford Davies' setting of Psalm 121, before the Dean of Canterbury read a moving passage from the Archbishop's Enthronement Sermon at Canterbury: 'The way of Jesus means reverencing people whether they belong to our party or not.' But in order that things did not get too solemn (after all the archbishop was a man with 'an engaging and infectious sense of humour') his son read a selection of Robert Runcie's favourite sayings by the early nineteenth-century clerical wit Sydney Smith. This was followed by the hymn 'O Jesus I have promised', which Bishop Runcie must have heard hundreds of times when conducting confirmations in the St Albans and Canterbury dioceses.

The address was by his long-serving chaplain, now Bishop of London, Richard Chartres. After the address the singing of a setting of the Creed written for the Liturgy of St John Chrysostom recalled the fact that, already before he became archbishop, Robert Runcie had had more first-hand acquaintance with the Orthodox Churches than any Archbishop of Canterbury since the seventh century. The prayers were said by two episcopal colleagues who had also been fellow members of the staff at Cuddesdon Theological College, after which the choir sang the carol 'Jesus Christ the apple tree'. The final congregational hymn was the evening hymn (which had also been sung at his funeral) 'The day thou gavest, Lord, is ended', the service concluding with a setting of the Aaronic Blessing by the Cambridge-based composer John Rutter. This ensured that the other half of Oxbridge, where Runcie had been on the staff at Westcott House, and Dean of Trinity Hall, was rightfully represented.

Westminster Abbey

A Service of Thanksgiving for the life and work of The Right Reverend and Right Honourable The Lord Runcie, MC

1921–2000

Archbishop of Canterbury

1980–1991

Wednesday 8 November 2000

ORDER OF SERVICE

All remain standing. The Collegiate Procession moves to places in the Quire and Sacrarium.

The Choir sings

THE INTROIT

Since by man came death by man came also the resurrection of the dead.

For as in Adam all die even so in Christ shall all be made alive.

George Frideric Handel (1685–1759)   *1 Corinthians 15.21–22*
from Messiah

All remain standing. The Very Reverend Dr Wesley Carr, Dean of Westminster, says

THE BIDDING

The rich variety of life represented in this congregation witnesses that today we thank God for a singular man: soldier and academic, Oxford graduate and Cambridge teacher, classical scholar and theologian; Anglican and ecumenist, bishop and archbishop, and not least husband and father. We remember before God Robert, archbishop and friend. He walked with the great yet watched for the humble in Church and State; in the Church of England and in the Anglican Communion; in Christian ecumenism and in the wider circle of faiths – all represented here today. But especially we praise God for so human a man, one who revelled in curiosity about the world – its history and culture, its problems and their solution – and who relished and sustained the many friendships that resulted.

We commend him to God, whom he faithfully served and simply loved. We pray for his family and all who especially feel bereaved. And let us also affirm for ourselves those abiding values for which Robert Runcie courageously stood.

All remain standing to sing

THE HYMN

Come down, O Love divine
NEH 137; AMNS 156; CP 175

Down Ampney   *Bianco da Siena (d 1434)*
Ralph Vaughan Williams (1872–1958)   *translated by* R F *Littledale*
                                                              (1833–90)

All sit. The Honourable Rebecca Tabor, Daughter, reads

PHILIPPIANS 4.1, 4–9

Hear the words of St Paul:

Therefore, my brothers and sisters, whom I love and long for, my joy
and crown, stand firm in the Lord in this way, my beloved. Rejoice in
the Lord always; again I will say, Rejoice. Let your gentleness be
known to everyone. The Lord is near. Do not worry about anything,
but in everything by prayer and supplication with thanksgiving let
your requests be made known to God. And the peace of God, which sur-
passes all understanding, will guard your hearts and your minds in
Christ Jesus. Finally, beloved, whatever is true, whatever is honourable,
whatever is just, whatever is pure, whatever is pleasing, whatever is com-
mendable, if there is any excellence and if there is anything worthy of
praise, think about these things. Keep on doing the things that you
have learned and received and heard and seen in me, and the God of
peace will be with you.

This is the word of the Lord.
Thanks be to God.

All remain seated. The Choir sings

PSALM 121
Henry Walford Davies (1869–1941)

*All remain seated. The Very Reverend John Simpson, Dean of Canterbury, from
the Nave Pulpit, says:*

Robert was a noted preacher, speaking with courage and always for the
faith. At Canterbury we were privileged to hear his first sermon as Archbishop, which included this passage. So for a moment, let us listen to
Robert, the Archbishop:

If the Church acts as if it possessed its answers to life's problems tied up in neat packages, it may be heard for a time. It may rally some waverers; but its influence will not last. It will confirm others in their suspicion and hostility. To them it will mean that the Church, like every other human institution, is making a bid for power.

I long to be able to speak, while archbishop, with men and women who stand outside the Christian Church. But I must stand also not at the edge but at the very centre of the Christian company as supporter and encourager – and my particular heroes among those who speak for Christ and follow his way are found in places where priest and people, men and women, of different ages, change the atmosphere of their local community, drawing people to Christ by the authority that their honesty and love and service win for them. This way of living and sharing, admitting our own failings and our longings, is not what people expect from those who sit on thrones. 'Speak out, condemn, denounce', is what is expected. But the throne of Jesus is a mercy-seat. It stands firm against all the vileness of the world but it stands also for compassion. The way of Jesus means reverencing people whether they belong to our party or not. The strategy of Jesus means changing lives with love.

Robert Runcie
Enthronement Sermon, Canterbury Cathedral, 1980

All remain seated. The Honourable James Runcie, from the Great Lectern, says:

My father held high office but remained thoroughly human. He made and valued friendships with people in all areas of life, and he had an engaging and infectious sense of humour, which helped nourish those friendships. Here is a short selection of some of his favourite sayings from Canon Sydney Smith.

'As the French say, there are three sexes – men, women, and clergy-men.'

'I love liberty, but hope that it can be managed that I shall have soft beds, good dinners, fine linen, etc. for the rest of my life.'

'You call me in your speech "my facetious friend", and I hasten to denominate you "my solemn friend"; but you and I must not run into common-place errors; you must not think me necessarily foolish because I am facetious, nor will I consider you necessarily wise because you are grave.'

'A squire once said to Sydney Smith: "If I had a son who was an idiot, by Jove, I'd make him a parson", to which he replied: "Very probably, but I see that your father was of a different mind".'

'Take short views, hope for the best, and trust in God.'

'I am, upon the whole, a happy man and have found the world an entertaining place, and am thankful to Providence for the part allotted to me in it.'

'We naturally lose illusions as we get older, like teeth, but there is no Cartwright to fit a new set into our understandings. I have, alas, only one illusion left, and that is the Archbishop of Canterbury.'

THE HYMN

O Jesus I have promised
NEH 420; AMNS 235; CP 538

Thornbury *John Bode (1816–74)*
Basil Harwood (1859–1949)

THE ADDRESS

by

The Right Reverend and Right Honourable Richard Chartres
Lord Bishop of London

Chaplain to Robert Runcie
St Albans 1975–80; Canterbury 1980–84

All remain seated. James Bowman, CBE, accompanied by the Choir sings

THE CREED

by

Alexandr Tikhonovich Grechaninov (1864–1956)
from the Divine Liturgy of St John Chrysostom, No. 2 op. 29

All kneel or sit for

THE PRAYERS

The Right Reverend Jim Thompson, Lord Bishop of Bath and Wells, says:

Let us pray:

O God our Father, we thank you for the promise of paradise. Help us to recover that vision, and, with your servant Robert and all your saints, receive us at the last into your heavenly kingdom, there to see you face to face; through Jesus Christ our Lord. **Amen.**

The Right Reverend Mark Santer, Lord Bishop of Birmingham, says:

Father of all, we give thanks for Robert's care for the common good, for his public witness to the values of justice, fairness and compassion, and in particular for *Faith in the City*. We recall with admiration his toughness under fire, both in war and in peace. We pray for all who are called to public office and service. Particularly we remember the Scots Guards. May they be faithful in service, strong in brotherhood, firm in defending the right and protected in all danger; through your Son, Jesus Christ our Lord. **Amen.**

The Bishop of Bath and Wells says:

O God of love, who knows and loves us as we are, we thank you for Robert, for his sense of fun, his humour and his humanity. We give thanks for his friendship, his love for family and friends, and for the way he made each person feel special. We bless you, Lord, for his quiet prayerfulness, for his ability to laugh at himself and for his keen sense of the ridiculous. Help us, who mourn his loss, to treasure our memories of him and find the friendly comfort of your Holy Spirit; through Jesus Christ our Lord. **Amen.**

The Bishop of Birmingham says:

Lord of the Church, we give you thanks for the gift of a wise and discerning pastor to your people. We remember his care for his fellow clergy, for religious and for ordinands. We thank you for the gift of his intellect, and for his commitment to the nurture of the human mind. So bless, we pray, our universities and schools and our places of theological study, bless the pastors of your Church in their ministry, and bless all your people in their discipleship, that the light of your truth in Christ may shine in all the world. For these and all your gifts we pray in the name of the Good Shepherd of all, your Son our Saviour Jesus Christ. **Amen.**

As we look for the coming of God's kingdom among us, let us pray in faith and trust:

Our Father, who art in heaven, hallowed be thy name. Thy kingdom come, thy will be done, on earth as it is in heaven. Give us this day our daily bread. And forgive us our trespasses, as we forgive those who trespass against us. And lead us not into temptation, but deliver us from evil; for thine is the kingdom, the power and the glory, for ever and ever, Amen.

All remain seated or kneeling. The Choir sings:

> The tree of life my soul hath seen,
> Laden with fruit, and always green:
> The trees of nature fruitless be
> Compared with Christ the apple tree.
>
> His beauty doth all things excel:
> By faith I know, but ne'er can tell
> The glory which I now can see
> In Jesus Christ the apple tree.
>
> For happiness I long have sought,
> And pleasure dearly I have bought:
> I missed of all; but now I see
> 'Tis found in Christ the apple tree.
>
> I'm weary with my former toil,
> Here I will sit and rest awhile:
> Under the shadow I will be,
> Of Jesus Christ the apple tree.
>
> This fruit doth make my soul to thrive,
> It keeps my dying faith alive;
> Which makes my soul in haste to be
> With Jesus Christ the apple tree.

Elizabeth Poston (1905–85)   *Anonymous, from the collection of Joshua Smith,*
New Hampshire (1784)

The Reverend Dominic Fenton, Precentor of Westminster Abbey, says:

Bring us, O Lord God, at our last awakening into the house and gate of heaven, to enter into that gate and dwell in that house, where there shall be no darkness nor dazzling, but one equal light; no noise nor silence, but one equal music; no fears nor hopes, but one equal possession; no ends nor beginnings, but one equal eternity: in the habitations of thy glory and dominion, world without end. **Amen.**

John Donne (1572–1631)

All stand to sing

THE HYMN

The day thou gavest, Lord, is ended
NEH 252; AMNS 16; CP 22

St Clement   *John Ellerton (1826–93)*
Clement Scholefield (1839–1904)

All remain standing. The Dean says

THE BLESSING

God grant to the living grace; to the departed rest; to the Church, the Queen, the Commonwealth and all mankind, peace and concord, and to us sinners, eternal life; and the blessing of God Almighty, the Father, the Son and the Holy Spirit, be upon you and remain with you always. **Amen.**

All remain standing. The Choir sings

The Lord bless you and keep you.
The Lord make his face to shine upon you, and be gracious unto you:
The Lord lift up the light of his countenance upon you, and give you
    peace. Amen.

John Rutter (b 1945)   *Numbers 6.24–26*

SERVICE AT DUNBLANE

Almost within the hour of the tragedy in their town people took refuge
in Dunblane's largest building, the cathedral. It's not a cathedral in the
English sense but a parish church of the national church, the Church of
Scotland. Andrew Barr, who was there for the BBC, has described how
someone was standing by the door of the cathedral for the simple and
sensible reason, that there was a step down to catch the unwary or
nervous visitor. That step was a godsend because the gentle spoken
warning 'careful the step' was an icebreaker for anyone in those first
dark days: 'Please take care and feel welcome.'

On that day of horror, 13 March 1996, the cathedral became one of the
few places of sanctuary where people realized they could feel safe to sit
in their bewilderment and shock. Here too, kind arms and hands were
held out – without words. People stopped in mid word to sob. The
organ alternated with the piano – played gently so that the silence was
not overbearing. Little gestures – packets of tissues on all the pews
gifted by the Salvation Army – answered practical needs.

By the Saturday evening (it was the day before Mothering Sunday)
flowers had arrived in almost unbearable number and fresh blooms
were piled high in every corner. A table was laden with little teddy
bears, a single candle burnt in the chancel and nearby 17 single roses lay
side by side with a small card containing the name of each child and
their teacher.

Is there a new understanding about flowers? It is suggested that the
flowers placed where a horrific or violent event has occurred are a way
in which we symbolize the driving out of evil from our own communities. The stadium, the school gate, the road sign become a sacred
space. By Saturday night the warm floodlit interior of Dunblane
Cathedral had been 'consecrated with flowers', to use Andrew Barr's
phrase.

In the light of this initial communal experience there could be no other
place for a memorial service than the cathedral; the service took place
seven months later on 9 October 1996. The result was the product of
much discussion, thought and prayer with the families and others concerned with the future in Dunblane. It focused on the theme of light,
built around the lighting of 17 candles as a remembrance of the children
and their teacher, but also expressing the important need to move on
from darkness to light. Even the service booklet made this point. The sil-
houette scene of the hills above Dunblane on the front cover has no
sun, but then each of the following pages has a gradually rising sun
until, on the final page, it is high in the sky.

After a welcome and a call to worship the congregation sang the children's hymn 'All things bright and beautiful'. Following prayers, Rutter's setting of a Gaelic Blessing was sung, leading into the Act of Remembrance. This section contained a specially written hymn by Jean Holloway, a reading of 'Little Child Lost' by Eugene G. Merryman Jr and a piper playing a Lament for Children outside the west door of the cathedral. A candle was brought forward, one for each of the children and their teacher, which was lit by family members and placed on a table at the crossing (the intersection of nave and transepts). Three short passages of scripture preceded a minute's silence and then a prayer and a hymn.

The scripture readings following the Act of Remembrance all reflected the theme of light and the sermon took as its text our Lord's words 'I am the light of the world'. After the sermon, and before the Benediction, all sang the popular 'Shine, Jesus, Shine'.

Out of Darkness into Light

A Memorial Service
for the sixteen children and
their teacher who died in the
Dunblane Primary School tragedy
on 13 March 1996

held in Dunblane Cathedral
on Wednesday 9 October 1996
at 2.30 pm

in the presence of His Royal Highness,
the Prince of Wales

ORDER OF SERVICE

Service conducted by
The Revd George G. Cringles (St Blane's Church)
The Revd William M. Gilmour (Lecropt Church)
The Revd Moira Herkes (Dunblane Cathedral)
Canon Basil O'Sullivan (Church of the Holy Family)
The Revd Colin G. McIntosh (Dunblane Cathedral)
Preacher: The Very Revd Professor James A. Whyte

Organist: Matthew Beetschen
Piper: Hugh McCallum

WELCOME AND CALL TO WORSHIP

PRAISE

Tune: All things bright and beautiful

All things bright and beautiful,
all creatures great and small,
all things wise and wonderful,
the Lord God made them all.

Each little flower that opens,
each little bird that sings,
He made their glowing colours,
He made their tiny wings.

The purple-headed mountain,
the river running by,
the sunset, and the morning
that brightens up the sky,

The cold wind in the winter,
the pleasant summer sun,
the ripe fruits in the garden,
He made them every one:

He gave us eyes to see them,
and lips that we might tell
how great is God Almighty,
who has made all things well.

Cecil Frances Alexander

CALL TO PRAYER
(Congregation Standing)

Prayers of Approach and Petition

A Gaelic Blessing   *John Rutter*

Deep peace of the running wave to you . . .

deep peace of the quiet earth to you . . .

deep peace of the shining stars to you . . .

deep peace of the gentle night to you . . .

moon and stars pour their healing light on you . . .

deep peace of Christ the light of the world to you.

AN ACT OF REMEMBRANCE

PRAISE

Tune: Melita
(Eternal Father, strong to save)

O Father, on your love we call,
when sorrow overshadows all,
and pain that feels too great to bear
drives from us any words for prayer;
enfold in love for evermore
all those we love, but see no more.

Our children, innocent and dear,
were strangers to a world of fear;
each precious life had more to give,
in each, our hopes and dreams could live;
enfold in love for evermore
all those we love, but see no more.

So brief, the joy since each was born,
so long the years in which to mourn;
give us compassion to sustain
each other in this time of pain;
    enfold in love for evermore
    all those we love, but see no more.

Guard us from bitterness and hate,
and share with us grief's crushing weight;
help us to live from day to day,
until, once more, we find our way;
    enfold in love for evermore
    all those we love, but see no more.

When dark despair is all around,
and falling tears the only sound,
light one small flame of hope that still
you walk with us, and always will
    enfold in love for evermore
    all those we love, but see no more.

Jean Holloway

READING – 'LITTLE CHILD LOST'

Shall we ever find anything other than a child that can be such a paradox in our lives? A little person that can generate such a conflict of anger and love. One that causes so much disappointment and pride at the same time. So much sorrow when they have been hurt only to cause so much happiness with their laughter.

One who can cause so much fear for their safety and well-being, cause so much comfort and serenity when they are asleep in your arms. This little person has the ability to pull at each and every emotion known to man and some that they are not even aware.

When the loss of this little person happens, no matter how, what do we do then? Will we ever escape the sound of their voice; does it still come from their room?

We will never quit catching a glimpse of them out of the corner of our eye. Was that my little one or just an illusion? Your answer is – you see and hear – just as you continue to love, for you see that child was a part of your soul. Although you may not always hear them, as they move upon the wings of the wind, nor may you always see them as they flash past on a ray of sunlight, be assured they are with you.

Though I may never be able to explain your loss or console you, I wish to thank you. For you see, without your child, and other children who have gone before us, there would be no children in heaven. Playing where they never tire, your child is safe and happy.

written by Eugene G. Merryman, Jnr
June 1995, France
copyright 95, Ka Ge Co.

read by Lorraine Kelly

THE LAMENT
Piper plays 'Lament for the Children'
Patrick Mor MacCrimmon

(A candle is lit for each of the sixteen children and their teacher as we remember their lives)

REMEMBERING THE CHILDREN

'Would God that I had died for thee, O Absalom my son, my son'

(2 Samuel 18.33)

'Truly, I say to you, unless you turn and become like children, you will never enter the kingdom of heaven. Whoever humbles himself like this child, he is the greatest in the kingdom of heaven'

(St Matthew 18.3–4)

REMEMBERING GWEN MAYOR

'I will teach you and guide you in the way you should go. I will counsel you and watch over you'

(Psalm 32.8)

ONE MINUTE SILENCE

PRAYER

The Gift of Tears

Lord, we give you thanks for the gift of tears:
for tears of grief, redeeming our mourning from despair;
for tears of anger, awakening our thirst for justice;
for tears of laughter, celebrating our joy in living.

May the light of Christ shining through our tears
become the rainbow of your promise,
shedding colours of your love's bright presence
in your grieving, struggling, laughing world.

PRAISE

Tune: Ye banks and braes

We cannot measure how you heal
    or answer every sufferer's prayer,
yet we believe your grace responds
    where faith and doubt unite to care.
Your hands, though bloodied on the cross,
    survive to hold and heal and warn,
to carry all through death to life
    and cradle children yet unborn.

The pain that will not go away,
    the guilt that clings from things long past,
the fear of what the future holds,
    are present as if meant to last.
But present too is love which tends
    the hurt we never hoped to find,
the private agonies inside,
    the memories that haunt the mind.

So some have come who need your help
    and some have come to make amends,
as hands which shaped and saved the world
    are present in the touch of friends.
Lord, let your Spirit meet us here
    to mend the body, mind and soul,
to disentangle peace from pain
    and make your broken people whole.

John Bell and Graham Maule

OLD TESTAMENT LESSON

Isaiah chapter 60, verses 1–3, 19–22

ANTHEM

Lux Aeterna

'May eternal light shine upon them, O Lord, with your saints for ever: because you are gracious'

composed by Robert Steadman on 14 March 1996

NEW TESTAMENT LESSON

1 John chapter 1, verses 5–9
Revelation chapter 22, verses 1–5

SERMON

When Jesus spoke again to the people, he said: 'I am the light of the world. Whoever follows me will not walk in darkness, but will have the light of life'

(St John 8.12)

PRAYERS OF COMMEMORATION AND INTERCESSION

PRAISE

Tune: Shine, Jesus, Shine

Lord the light of your love is shining
in the midst of the darkness, shining.
    Jesus light of the world shine upon us,
    set us free by the truth you now bring us.
Shine on me, shine on me.

Shine, Jesus, shine,
    fill this land with the Father's glory,
blaze, Spirit, blaze,
    set our hearts on fire.

Flow, river, flow,
flood the nations with grace and mercy,
send forth your word, Lord,
and let there be light.

Lord, I come to your awesome presence,
from the shadows into your radiance;
by the blood I may enter your brightness,
search me – try me – consume all my darkness.
Shine on me, shine on me.

As we gaze on your kingly brightness
so our faces display your likeness,
ever changing from glory to glory,
mirrored here may our lives tell your story.
Shine on me, shine on me.

Graham Kendrick

BENEDICTION AND CHORAL AMEN

(At the end of the Service the Congregation is asked to remain seated until the
Prince of Wales and the immediate members of the bereaved families have left the
Cathedral.)

Our Children: Victoria Clydesdale
Emma Crozier
Melissa Currie
Charlotte Dunn
Kevin Hasell
Ross Irvine
David Kerr
Mhairi McBeath
Brett McKinnon
Abigail McLennan
Emily Morton
Sophie North
John Petrie
Joanna Ross
Hannah Scott
Megan Turner
Their Teacher: Gwen Mayor

I am standing on the seashore. A ship in the bay lifts her anchor, spreads her white sails to the morning breeze and starts out upon the ocean.

She is an object of beauty and strength, and I stand and watch her until she hangs like a speck of white cloud just where the sea and sky mingle with each other. Then someone at my side says, 'She's gone!' Gone where! Gone from view, that is all.
Just at that moment there are other eyes watching her coming and other souls taking up the glad shout, 'There, she's coming!'

AND THAT IS DYING

MARCHIONESS MEMORIAL SERVICE

Among the shocking facts of the *Marchioness* disaster was that it took place in the middle of a busy and energetic city, and that it involved a group of fun-loving young people who were in the midst of enjoying themselves on an evening pleasure trip on the River Thames.

Southwark Cathedral stands hard by the Thames; and was the natural place for a memorial service for those who died on the river on the night of Sunday, 20 August 1989. The service which is included in this chapter is the one which was held immediately after the disaster. Yet Southwark Cathedral has kept faith with those who still grieve the loss of loved ones on that terrible night. Twelve months after the tragedy another service was held in the cathedral, and on the tenth anniversary there was also a 'Service of Thanksgiving' at which a candle was lit for each of the 51 victims.

The service immediately after the disaster was fully ecumenical, with both the Archbishop of Canterbury and the Archbishop of Westminster taking part. After an opening hymn ('God is Love'), and an introduction by the Provost of Southwark, the congregation sang the metrical version of the twenty-third psalm before the Archbishop of Canterbury's sermon.

The choir anthem by John Ireland was a setting of words from the Song of Solomon. These verses included part of the inscription which had been carved on the memorial stone due to be dedicated at the close of the service: 'Many waters cannot quench love'.

Prayers for the emergency services and the Thames river boat fraternity followed, to which the Cardinal Archbishop added an ascription.

After a hymn by Cardinal Newman there was the reading of a catena of suitable scriptural passages. The next series of prayers were shared by the Cardinal Archbishop and the Superintendent Minister of Westminster Methodist Central Hall. Within these prayers there was a period of silence for remembrance and the singing, by the choir, of the Russian Contakion of the Departed.

The cathedral had moved quickly and their stonemasons had produced a memorial of black granite. Already the quotation from the Song of Solomon had been carved out and the promise given that the names of the victims would subsequently be inscribed. This stone was then dedicated by the Bishop of Southwark. As part of the ceremony the Lord Mayor of London and the Mayor of Southwark read from St John's Gospel. The final hymn, before the Archbishop's blessing, was an Easter hymn of hope 'The strife is o'er, the battle done'.

Service after the Disaster
on the River Thames,
Southwark Cathedral

ORDER OF SERVICE

At 12 noon the Congregation stands and the Procession of the Choir, the Clergy, the Bishops and the Archbishops enters.

HYMN

God is Love: let heaven adore him
NEH 364; AMNS 365; CP 442

Timothy Rees (1874–1939)

Sit

INTRODUCTION
Read by the Provost

For about a thousand years this church has stood by the river. Today it is our privilege to offer what we can in order to share the grief and the prayers of those who mourn after the tragedy of the sinking of the Motor Vessel *Marchioness*. One of the ancient docks near this church is named after St Mary, the mother of Jesus, and today we may recall what was said about her grief: 'A sword shall pierce your heart'. Another of the old docks on this South Bank of the Thames is named St Saviour's, for this is the church of the Saviour and St Mary. The Saviour is Jesus Christ, who has conquered death and all forms of darkness. Our Lord invited us to accept the eternal light and love of God our Heavenly Father. He says: 'Blessed are those who mourn, for they shall be comforted'.

Stand

HYMN

The Lord's my shepherd, I'll not want
NEH 459; AMNS 426; CP 594

Psalm 23 in the Scottish Psalter (1650)

Sit

SERMON
by the Archbishop of Canterbury

ANTHEM

The Choir sings the Anthem by John Ireland (1879–1962). The first words, taken from the Song of Solomon in the Old Testament, are carved on the Memorial Stone to be dedicated later in the service.

Minister:

We give thanks for the response of the Emergency Services and we pray for them.

O Heavenly Father, who by your son Jesus Christ taught us the glory of self-sacrifice: Bless all who are called to serve in the Police, in the Ambulance and Social Services, in the Fire Brigade and in the Hospitals. May they always remember that they are fellow workers with you and the instruments of your love. Make them strong and gentle, upright and compassionate, in the way of the cross of our Leader and Redeemer. **Amen**

We pray for the River Boat Fraternity.

Eternal Lord God, the Creator of the rivers and the seas, whose Son our Saviour called fishermen to be his first disciples: Guide all who work on the River Thames, that through their skills and constant devotion to duty the people and the commerce of this City may be conveyed in safety, until we come in eternity to the ocean of your pure and unbounded love; through Jesus Christ our Lord. **Amen**

As our Saviour taught us, so we pray

All:

> **Our Father in heaven,**
> **hallowed be your name**
> **your kingdom come,**
> **your will be done,**
> **on earth as in heaven.**
> **Give us today our daily bread.**
> **Forgive us our sins**
> **as we forgive those who sin against us.**
> **Lead us not into temptation,**
> **but deliver us from evil.**
> **For the kingdom, the power, and the glory are yours,**
> **now and for ever.** **Amen**

Cardinal:

To him who is able to keep us from falling, and to present us faultless before the presence of his glory with exceeding joy, to the only wise God our Saviour, be glory and majesty, dominion and power, both now and ever. **Amen**

Jude 24, 25

Stand

HYMN

Praise to the holiest in the height
NEH 439; AMNS 117; CP 557

J. H. Newman (1801–90)

Many waters cannot quench love, neither can the floods drown it. Love is strong as death. Greater love hath no man than this, that a man lay down his life for his friends. Who his own self bare our sins in his own body on the tree, that we, being dead to sins, should live unto righteousness. Ye are washed, ye are sanctified, ye are justified in the Name of the Lord Jesus; ye are a chosen generation, a royal priesthood, a holy nation, that ye should shew forth the praises of him who hath called you out of darkness into his marvellous light. I beseech you, brethren, by the mercies of God, that ye present your bodies, a living sacrifice, holy, acceptable unto God, which is your reasonable service.

Kneel or sit

PRAYERS

Read by Cardinal Basil Hume, Archbishop of Westminster, and the Minister of the Methodist Central Hall, Westminster.

Cardinal:

>   The Lord is full of compassion and mercy:
>   slow to anger and of great goodness.
>   As a father is tender towards his children:
>   so is the Lord tender to those that fear him.

Psalm 103.8, 13

The eternal God is your refuge, and underneath are the everlasting arms.

Deuteronomy 33.27

Neither death, nor life, nor angels, nor principalities, nor powers, nor things present, nor things to come, nor height, nor depth, nor anything else in all creation will be able to separate us from the love of God in Christ Jesus our Lord.

Romans 8.38, 39

We entrust into the merciful keeping of God, their Creator, Redeemer and Sanctifier, the souls of those whom we remember today.

A period of silence is kept for remembrance.

O Father of all, we pray to you for those whom we love, but see no longer. Grant them your peace; let light perpetual shine upon them; and in your loving wisdom and almighty power work in them the good purpose of your perfect will, through Jesus Christ our Lord. **Amen**

Bring us, O Lord God, at our last awakening into the house and gate of heaven, to enter into that gate and dwell in that house, where there shall be no darkness nor dazzling, but one equal light; no noise nor silence, but one equal music; no fears nor hopes, but one equal possession; no ends nor beginnings, but one equal eternity; in the habitations of thy glory and dominion, world without end. **Amen**

The Choir sings the Russian Contakion of the Departed

Give rest, O Christ, to thy sevant with thy Saints: where sorrow and pain are no more; neither sighing, but life everlasting. Thou only art immortal, the Creator and Maker of man: and we are mortal, formed of the earth, and unto earth shall we return: for so thou didst ordain, when thou createdst me, saying, Dust thou art, and unto dust shalt thou return. All we go down to the dust; and weeping o'er the grave, we make our song: Alleluya, Alleluya, Alleluya.

Cardinal:

We pray for those who survive and mourn, that all may know the comfort of God's presence amid grief.

Father in heaven, you gave your Son Jesus Christ to suffering and to death on the cross, and raised him to life in glory. Grant us a patient faith in time of darkness, and strengthen our hearts with the knowledge of your love. **Amen**

O Lord grant us the light of your Spirit, that we may live more bravely and faithfully for your sake and for the sake of those who are no longer with us here on earth; and enable us so to serve you day by day that we may find eternal fellowship with them in you; through him who died and rose again for us all, your Son Jesus Christ, our Saviour. **Amen**

DEDICATION OF THE MEMORIAL STONE

by the Bishop of Southwark

Stand

Bishop:

My tears have been my food day and night: while they ask me all day long, 'where now is your God?'

All:

> **As I pour out my soul by myself**
> **I remember this:**
> **how I went to the house of the Mighty One,**
> **into the temple of God.**

Psalm 42.3, 4

Bishop:

In the faith of Jesus Christ crucified and risen from the dead, and in perpetual remembrance of those who lost their lives in this tragedy, we dedicate this Stone to the glory of God, Father, Son and Holy Spirit. **Amen**

Bishop:

The Lord God will swallow up death for ever.

All:

> **He will wipe away the tears from every face.**

Isaiah 25.8

Sit

PSALM 121

Sung by the Choir

I will lift up mine eyes unto the hills: from whence cometh my help?

LESSONS

Read by the Lord Mayor:

Let not your heart be troubled: ye believe in God, believe also in me. In my Father's house are many mansions: if it were not so, I would have told you. I go to prepare a place for you. And if I go and prepare a place for you, I will come again, and receive you unto myself; that where I am, there ye may be also. And whither I go ye know, and the way ye know. Thomas saith unto him, Lord, we know not whither thou goest, and how can we know the way? Jesus saith unto him, I am the way, the truth, and the life.

John 14.1–6

Read by the Mayor of Southwark:

Many came to Martha and Mary, to comfort them concerning their brother. Then Martha, as soon as she heard that Jesus was coming, went and met him: but Mary sat still in the house. Then said Martha unto Jesus, Lord, if thou hadst been here, my brother had not died. But I know, that even now, whatsoever thou wilt ask of God, God will give it thee. Jesus saith unto her, Thy brother shall rise again. Martha saith unto him, I know that he shall rise again in the resurrection at the last day. Jesus said unto her, I am the resurrection, and the life: he that believeth in me, though he were dead, yet shall he live; and whosoever liveth and believeth in me shall never die.

John 11.19–26

Stand

HYMN

The strife is o'er, the battle done
NEH 119; AMNS 78; CP 159

17th century, translated by Francis Pott (1832–1909)

Kneel or sit

BLESSING
by the Archbishop of Canterbury

Archbishop:

Rest eternal grant unto them, O Lord.

All:

And let light perpetual shine upon them.

Archbishop:

The peace of God, which passes all understanding, keep your hearts and minds in the knowledge and love of God, and of his Son Jesus Christ our Lord; and the blessing of God almighty, the Father, the Son, and the Holy Spirit, be among you, and remain with you always. **Amen**

COMMON WORSHIP OUTLINES

AN OUTLINE ORDER FOR A MEMORIAL SERVICE FROM *COMMON WORSHIP*

The Gathering
1 The minister welcomes the people and introduces the service.
2 Sentences of Scripture may be used.
3 Authorized Prayers of Penitence may be used.
4 The Collect may be said here or in the Prayers.

Readings and Sermon
5 One or more readings from the Bible is used.
  Psalms or hymns may follow the readings.
6 Other songs and readings may be used and a tribute or tributes made.
7 A sermon is preached, testimony may be given and an authorized Creed or Affirmation of Faith may be used.

Prayers
8 The prayers usually follow this sequence:
- Thanksgiving for the life of the departed
- Prayer for those who mourn
- Prayers of Penitence (if not already used)
- Prayer for readiness to live in the light of eternity

Commendation and Dismissal
The dead person is commended to God with authorized words. The service may end with a blessing.

AN OUTLINE ORDER FOR A MEMORIAL SERVICE WITHIN A CELEBRATION OF HOLY COMMUNION

The Gathering
1 The minister welcomes the people and introduces the service.
2 Sentences of Scripture may be used.
3 Authorized Prayers of Penitence are used here or in the Prayers.
4 The Collect is said here or in the Prayers.

The Liturgy of the Word

5 One or more readings from the Bible, including a Gospel reading, is used.
Psalms or hymns may follow the readings.

6 Other songs and readings may be used and a tribute or tributes made.

7 A sermon is preached, testimony may be given and an authorized Creed or Affirmation of Faith may be used.

Prayers

8 The prayers usually follow this sequence:
- Thanksgiving for the life of the departed
- Prayer for those who mourn
- Prayers of Penitence (if not already used)
- Prayer for readiness to live in the light of eternity

The Liturgy of the Sacrament

9 The Peace

10 Preparation of the Table
Taking of the Bread and Wine

11 The Eucharistic Prayer (any authorized Eucharistic Prayer may be used)

12 The Lord's Prayer (used here rather than in the Prayers)

13 Breaking of the Bread

14 Giving of Communion

15 Prayer after Communion

Commendation and Dismissal

16 The dead person is commended to God with authorized words.

17 The service may end with a blessing.

NOTES

1 These Outline Orders are designed for use in church several weeks after the Funeral service has taken place.

2 If the memorial service takes place on the same day as, or very soon after, the Funeral, the Funeral service should be used, without the Committal.

3 For annual memorial services a provision such as that on pages 62–82 in *The Promise of His Glory* should be used.

4 Care should be taken to ensure that there is a clear president throughout, who introduces and concludes the service, and that the number of other speakers, musical items and non-biblical readings does not unbalance the service from its focus on the word of God, prayer and thanksgiving.

These orders are reprinted from *Common Worship: Pastoral Services*, pp. 331–4.

References

Sources for Memorial Service Material

Benn, June (ed.), *Memorials: An Anthology of Poetry and Prose*, Ravette, Partridge Green, 1986.

Benson, Judi and Falk, Agneta (eds), *The Long Pale Corridor: Contemporary Poems of Bereavement*, Bloodaxe Books, Northumberland, 1996.

Bentley, James, Bell, Andrew and Hunt, Jackie (eds), *Funerals: A Guide. Prayers, Readings and Hymns*, Hodder & Stoughton, London, 1994.

Remembrance: An Anthology of Readings, Prayers and Music Chosen for Memorial Services (Introduced by Ned Sherrin, Foreword by the Archbishop of Canterbury), Michael Joseph, London, 1996.

Whitaker, Agnes (ed.), *All in the End is Harvest: An Anthology for those who Grieve*, Darton, Longman & Todd, London, 1984.

You are reminded that increasingly prayer material is available on the Internet. For example: www.cofe.anglican.org/commonworship or www.cptryon.org/prayer.

Select Bibliography

Bennett, Alan, *The Laying on of Hands: A Story*, Profile Books in association with *London Review of Books*, London, 2001.

Common Worship: Pastoral Services, Church House Publishing, London, 2000.

Cope, Gilbert (ed.), *Dying, Death and Disposal*, SPCK, London, 1970.

Davies, Douglas J., *Death, Ritual and Belief: The Rhetoric of Funerary Rites*, Cassell, London, 1997.

Edwards, David L., *After Death? Past Beliefs and Real Possibilities*, Contemporary Christian Insights, Continuum, London, 2001.

Guidelines for Best Practice of Clergy at Funerals, The Churches' Funerals Group, London, 1997.

Guidelines for Faith Communities when Dealing with Disasters, Church of England Board for Social Responsibility, London, 1997.

Horton, R. Anne, *Using Common Worship: Funerals, A Practical Guide to the New Services*, Church House Publishing, London, 2000.

Jupp, Peter C. and Rogers, Tony (eds), *Interpreting Death: Christian Theology and Pastoral Practice*, Cassell, London, 1997.

Memorial Services, Alcuin Pamphlets VI, Mowbray, London, 1914.

Perham, Michael, *New Handbook of Pastoral Liturgy*, SPCK, London, 2000.

The Promise of His Glory: Services and Prayers for the Season from All Saints' to Candle-mas, Church House Publishing/Mowbray, London, 1991.

Rowell, D. Geoffrey, *The Liturgy of Christian Burials*, Alcuin Club Collections, LIX, SPCK, London, 1977.

Rutherford, H. Richard, *Honouring the Dead*, The Liturgical Press, Collegeville, Minnesota, 2001.

Rutherford, Richard with Barr, Tony, *The Death of a Christian: The Order of Christian Funerals*, revised edition, A Pueblo Book, The Liturgical Press, Collegeville, Minnesota, 1990.

Wolffe, John, *Great Deaths: Grieving, Religion, and Nationhood in Victorian and Edwardian Britain*, British Academy Postdoctoral Fellowship Monograph, Oxford University Press, Oxford, 2000.

Wyatt, E. G. P., *The Burial Service*, Alcuin Club Pamphlet VII, Mowbray, London, 1918.

Index

The Society for Promoting Christian Knowledge (SPCK) was founded in 1698. Its mission statement is:

To promote Christian knowledge by

- **Communicating the Christian faith in its rich diversity**
- **Helping people to understand the Christian faith and to develop their personal faith; and**
- **Equipping Christians for mission and ministry**

SPCK Worldwide serves the Church through Christian literature and communication projects in 100 countries, and provides books for those training for ministry in many parts of the developing world. This worldwide service depends upon the generosity of others and all gifts are spent wholly on ministry programmes, without deductions.

SPCK Bookshops support the life of the Christian community by making available a full range of Christian literature and other resources, providing support for those training for ministry, and assisting bookstalls and book agents throughout the UK.

SPCK Publishing produces Christian books and resources, covering a wide range of inspirational, pastoral, practical and academic subjects. Authors are drawn from many different Christian traditions, and publications aim to meet the needs of a wide variety of readers in the UK and throughout the world.

The Society does not necessarily endorse the individual views contained in its publications, but hopes they stimulate readers to think about and further develop their Christian faith.

For information about the Society, visit our website at *www.spck.org.uk*, or write to:
SPCK, Holy Trinity Church, Marylebone Road,
London NW1 4DU, United Kingdom.